BLACKS IN THE AMERICAN WEST

Editors

Richard Newman

Marcia Renée Sawyer

The involvement of blacks at every point in the exploration, history, and ongoing life of the American West remains a little-known story. The books—both fiction and nonfiction—in this series aim to preserve these stories and to celebrate the achievement and culture of early African-American westerners.

BORN TO BE

BY
TAYLOR GORDON

With an Introduction by Muriel Draper
a Foreword by Carl Van Vechten
and Illustrations by
Covarrubias
❧

Introduction to the Bison Books Edition
by Thadious M. Davis

University of Nebraska Press
Lincoln and London

Introduction to the Bison Books Edition © 1995 by the University of
Nebraska Press
Manufactured in the United States of America

♾ The paper in this book meets the minimum requirements of
American National Standard for Information Sciences—Perma-
nence of Paper for Printed Library Materials, ANSI Z39.48-1984.

First Bison Books printing: 1995
Most recent printing indicated by the last digit below:
10   9   8   7   6   5   4   3   2   1

Library of Congress Cataloging-in-Publication Data
Gordon, Taylor, 1893–1971.
Born to be / by Taylor Gordon; with an introduction by Muriel
Draper; a foreword by Carl Van Vechten; and illustrations by
Covarrubias; introduction to the Bison Books ed. by Thadious M.
Davis.
p.   cm.—(Blacks in the American West)
Previously published: Seattle: University of Washington Press, 1975.
ISBN 0-8032-7052-6 (pbk.)
1. Gordon, Taylor, 1893–1971.   2. Afro-Americans—Biography.
3. Afro-American singers—Biography.   I. Title.   II. Series.
E185.97.G66A3   1996
973'.0496073'0092—dc20
[B]
95-23534   CIP

Originally published in 1929 by Civici, Friede Inc., New York.

CONTENTS

v

CONTENTS

ILLUSTRATIONS

INTRODUCTION TO THE BISON BOOKS EDITION

COMPLETING THE CIRCLE: TAYLOR GORDON'S RETURN TO THE WEST

Thadious M. Davis

In 1929 when Taylor Gordon's *Born to Be* was published, it was part of a wave of books with what we now call "crossover appeal."[1] The autobiography of an African American whose particular achievement was in singing spirituals during the 1920s probably attracted a New York publisher because the Harlem Renaissance fostered a cross-racial interest in "things Negro."[2] With a foreword by Carl Van Vechten, who promoted the New Negro cultural movement both socially and professionally, and an introduction by Muriel Draper, who followed the interracial arts circuit in fashionable New York (and edited Gordon's manuscript), *Born to Be* drew a volley of well-placed reviews.[3] The nine original illustrations by Miguel Covarrubias, emphasizing the raciality of the subjects in caricature style, also contributed to the popular success of the autobiography as one of the "in" books of 1929.[4] And certainly Taylor Gordon's own flamboyant personality was a major factor in attracting attention to the book's racial component, for as Van Vechten states in his foreword: "It is a type of personality that many writers have tried to express . . . but no one has been entirely successful until Taylor Gordon somehow got himself on paper, lanky six-feet, falsetto voice, molasses laugh, and all the rest of him. . . ."

Yet Gordon's narrative is not a typical tale of growing up black in a race-conscious society and of achieving success in spite of the odds against people of color; for example, one of his initial self-descriptions reads: "I had reached the point in life where all boys wanted to be men. I acted as much so as possible. I got high-heeled boots, a six-horse-roll on my pants, leather cuffs,

Stetson hat, with a package of Bull Durham tobacco in my breast pocket and let the tag hang out, always chewing a match in company." Gordon images himself as a man in the gear and posture of a "cowboy"; indeed, he recounts learning to ride, drive, brand, and dehorn cattle, while hearing "cowboy songs and many a tale of the wild and wooly West" (42–43). Instead of the expected descriptions and incidents in the early life of a member of a racially homogeneous and segregated group, Gordon's autobiography offers the anecdotal, often amusing story of "Snowball," a child of the lone black family in a wide-open western mining town at the turn of the century.

"Snowball" is just one of the many nicknames that Emmanuel Taylor Gordon would acquire in the largely egalitarian town of White Sulphur Springs, Montana. He also answered to "Mannie," as well as to "Old Zip" and "Blackie," while growing up in Montana. Neither "Snowball" nor "Blackie" are racial slurs, because, as he earnestly observes, another member of his childhood circle was also nicknamed "Blackie," and the only thing black about him was his hair. The race-neutrality of Gordon's native environment and its polyglot community is one of the thematic cores of his autobiography. "What a lucky bird I am," he concludes, "to have been laid on top of the Rocky Mountains, hatched out by the Broiling Sun, a suckling of Honey Bluebacks and educated by the Grizzly Bear, with all the beauty and fresh air nature can provide for her children" (234).

Born 29 April 1893 in White Sulphur Springs, Taylor Gordon spent his childhood in the Smith River valley of the Rocky Mountains. While his representation of his early life as the youngest child of a laundress is not idyllic, for the Gordons were poor and hardworking, it nonetheless fuels a myth of harmony within ethnic diversity, of spiritual innocence amid physical pleasures. In the mixture of peoples in White Sulphur, from gamblers and prostitutes to sheep ranchers and miners, Gordon maps a rough but simultaneously protective world in which race is not a debilitating factor. As he recalls: "I knew I was black and different in appearance from most of the kids I played with, but my being so never changed the values of the game we might be playing. I got a chance to pitch or bat at the time my merits won for me either of the positions" (233). In the meritocracy that Gordon remembers, racism and racial hierarchies are nonexistent, yet his text is not, as Muriel Draper maintains in her introduction, "as free of racial self-consciousness as it is of literary self-consciousness." His varied accounts of working as a messenger for the local houses on the line (brothels), as a pin setter in a bowling alley, as a pipe cleaner and opium seller in an opium den, as an automobile driver and mechanic, as a derrick and rake operator on a farm, and as a riding hand on cattle drives—all forward the conception that within the still fluid social categories of the West, race was not an issue, but that he was very much aware of himself as racially marked.

Gordon left Montana for the first time at the age of seventeen when he traveled to St. Paul, Minnesota, to work as a chauffeur. Although he had spent a brief period in Helena, Montana, a city of about twelve thousand after the turn of the century, Gordon preferred to return to White Sulphur when he realized that Helena was too much like his own small town where everyone knew everyone else. For a youth with the sense of adventure that so clearly marked his identity, Gordon believed that the Montana "towns," including Butte, lacked allure and that the West was not the place for him. Moreover, once he witnessed firsthand the "power and conviction" of Easterners with money—such as the circus impresario and businessman John Ringling, who employed him as chauffeur for his land development company, Gordon "made up [his] mind then that the West was fine, but [he] wanted to be an Easterner" (55). His recognition of displacement at home and his desire for adventure propelled him to seek a future in the East.

However, in his description of leaving White Sulphur Springs on 11 September 1910 for St. Paul and a job as a chauffeur, Gordon reminds us of his socialization in the frontier-like spaces of the Rockies:

> While looking out of the window of the day coach, watching the
> blue peaks of the Rockies disappear behind me, my mind turned
> to the last instructions Mother and friend had given me. Many of
> them I neglected, but one thing Mother told me I heeded, that I
> didn't need my forty-five in the city, so I had left it behind. Why?
> The thought came to me as the train rambled farther and farther
> from home, and I began to feel alone. I always felt safe anywhere
> with Blue Steel Betty by my side: she gave me courage and protec-
> tion at home when I was alone. They had pictured nothing but
> trouble in the city, still they convinced me that my forty-five would
> mean the worst. My nerves grew shaky. (65)

Without Blue Steel Betty, his forty-five revolver, on his hip for
company and security, Gordon feels vulnerable and alone. The
suspicion of difference in handling threats or trouble—that is,
without his Blue Steel Betty—unnerves him more than his
mother's predictions of "sickness, starvation, jail, even death"
outside of Montana. The gun, like the horse, is an emblem of
Gordon's life in the West. "Had I been on a saddle-horse at that
moment," Gordon recalls, "I might have turned back" (64–65).
The eastbound Chicago, Milwaukee and St. Paul Railroad train
is no horse, no subject to his bidding, but is a machine bound
to elaborate time tables and operational schedules and to fixed
routes and stops. Moreover, the railroad signifies mass mobility
and large-scale transformation of the North American continent.
The contrast between the individual's control over his horse
(and therefore his own mobility) and the lack of control in a
world of mechanical vehicles (and thus undifferentiated mass
positionality) marks Gordon's awareness of himself as a Westerner, and ultimately as an outsider to the racial communities
of blacks in the East: "In all and all, I convinced myself that my
people were as hard to figure out as perpetual motion" (173).

The markers of Gordon's identity are not, then, skin color
and the physical appearance of a black person, but rather the
behavioral patterns and familiar conduct of the West. His farewell to Montana is a paean to the special character of a place:

I mumbled to myself, Good-bye, sharp tops and deep canyons. I may never see you again, nor the heavy foliage that covers you, painted different hues by the rising and setting sun. No more shall I see the speckled trout hit at a fly-hook from behind a twig in rushing waters, or taste their delicious flesh, when it comes curling fried from a hot rock. I shall miss the bark of the pistol and the thud of a bullet when it brings down a blue grouse. I wondered if they rolled blue grouse in mud, feathers and all, then baked them in hot ashes in the city. (65–66)

Gordon knows the answer, but he codifies growing up in the West in terms of the landcape and his activities within that landscape—activities that cannot be duplicated within a cityscape.

To situate Taylor Gordon as a Westerner whose identity was irrevocably shaped by White Sulphur Springs, Montana, is not to deny his modern subjectivity, but it is both to claim his western formative experiences as a major component of his social life and to assert his psychological and social agency. Gordon is, of course, autonomous and individuated, but he is also socially determined, not only by the categories of race and gender, but also by the categories of group and community; that is, in particular, by the Westerners inhabiting White Sulphur, who though diverse in class and ethnicity, are connected in their social relations. He self-consciously positions himself as a racial other and cultural outsider, so that at once both white and black Easterners observe themselves captured in his bemused and unempathetic lens. Gordon's gaze constructs a social world always located just beyond full comprehension; for example, his chapter entitled "My People" interrogates arbitrary relations between races by means of Gordon's "scientific" interests and his "western" ideology.

The narrative resonates nonetheless with Gordon's exuberant spirit whether he is recounting mishaps or successes in Montana, Minnesota, New York, or Florida, or in France, England, Barbados, or St. Vincent. In London, for instance, he displays the same boundless enthusiasm in meeting Lady Astor and members of the British aristocracy as in encountering Florence Mills and the cast of *Blackbirds*. Despite his several failed attempts at romance, and the erasure of erotic desire in his representation of heterosexual relations, he invariably inserts tantalizing vignettes of the potential for a happy love affair.

In the face of frequent unemployment or almost constant underemployment, Gordon manages to display resiliency and hope. Rarely is his optimism darkened by his position in the social hierarchy or labor force. (He is most pessimistic, and oblique, when he considers his chances for marriage.) Straightforwardly, he constructs a narrative that remains constant in its insistence on the necessity of viable work opportunities, on the paucity of such opportunities, and thus on the absence of upward mobility in his life. Despite a creative partnership with J. Rosamund Johnson that began in 1925, took him on a concert tour of Europe in 1927, and enabled him to perform throughout the United States, Gordon did not achieve a lasting career as a singer. David Levering Lewis labels him "a very dark decadent" who used "his roguish personality" to captivate "white admirers." Levering continues: "Spontaneous, amoral, irreverent, yet respectful, always ready with a song or an outrageous remark about his own race, to much of Park Avenue and the Village he was everything Roland Hayes or Paul Robeson was—irritatingly—not."[5] And, in fact, Arnold Rampersad refers to Gordon merely as an "irreverent entertainer."[6] From about 1925 to the end of the decade, Gordon did provide the entertainment for Van Vechten's parties; he was a fixture on the list of guests most likely to enliven any uptown or downtown New York gathering; and he did reside rent-free in the "Dark Tower," A'Lelia Walker's Harlem limestone mansion on 136th Street that Zora Neale Hurston immortalized as Niggerati Manor. Nevertheless, using his fine tenor voice, he also earned a living and visibility by singing spirituals in recitals with J. Rosamond Johnson; for instance, through his highly publicized concerts at Town Hall in 1925[7] and his acclaimed concert at Carnegie Hall, sponsored by the Urban League, 13 February 1927.

Although in 1929 Van Vechten compared Taylor Gordon to Jim in Mark Twain's *Adventures of Huckleberry Finn*, contemporary readers may evoke a different literary association. From today's perspective, it seems clear that, like F. Scott Fitzgerald in *The Great Gatsby* (1925), Gordon explores in *Born to Be* the relationship between East and West—between the small mountain community of White Sulphur Springs, Montana, and the large urban areas of Chicago in the Midwest and New York in the East. His own movement east is marked by a complicated innocence personified by a Jay Gatsby, but rarely racialized. It is also marked by the transformation of the pastoral, pre-industrial setting of the isolated western community by the trains, automobiles, and machinery of modern techology impinging upon its serenity. That Gordon earned his way across country as automobile driver, driving instructor, and rail-car steward (cook, porter, and valet on John Ringling's private railroad car) speaks to his position within a modern and changing economy.

Born to Be is Taylor Gordon's only published book, but his life after the autobiography was not an immediate dive into obscurity. In June 1932, he traveled to Moscow with a group of twenty-two young African Americans, including Langston Hughes and Dorothy West, who were to produce a film for the Meschrabpom Film Corporation on the "exploitation" of blacks in the United States.[8] In 1934, his essay, "Malicious Lies Magnifying the Truth," appeared in Nancy Cunard's anthology *Negro*. He also performed in a few theatrical productions during the 1930s. Robert Hemenway identifies the following list of Gordon's stage work: Heywood Broun's Broadway review, *Shoot the Works;* Fred Astaire's musical, *Gay Divorce;* Lawrence Langner's *The Pursuit of Happiness.* In the early 1930s, Gordon claimed to have written a novel, "A Darky's Dream," and a short story collection, "Catchin Some Air," but neither has surfaced.[9] In addition, he pursued the interest in science and invention mentioned as his early ambition in *Born to Be* by inventing and selling toys, one of which, a "Tom Tom Toy," links Gordon to Ralph Ellison's portrait in *Invisible Man* of a tragic Depression-era character,

Todd Clifton, who sells Sambo dolls in Harlem. All of Taylor Gordon's efforts to make money and become fully self-sufficient were ultimately unproductive, as he admitted to Van Vechten: "I have tried every honest thing I know and no money or work is for me to have at present."[10]

Marshall Berman maintains:

> The innate dynamism of the modern economy, and of the culture that grows from this economy, annihilates everything that it creates—physical environments, social institutions, metaphysical ideas, artistic visions, moral values—in order to create more, to go on endlessly creating the world anew. This drive draws all modern men and women into its orbit, and forces us all to grapple with the question of what is essential, what is meaningful, and what is real in the maelstrom in which we move and live.[11]

Within this process of modern annihilation and creation, perhaps, lies a clue to interpreting Taylor Gordon's private maelstrom—the mental stress that is only implied in the autobiography of the 1920s, but that reconstitutes itself as a major breakdown in the 1940s. In the last portion of *Born to Be,* Gordon takes on philosophical issues, and these begin to reveal the "cracks" in his armor, the weak part of his defense against the constant onslaught of hunger, fear, unemployment, and uncertainty. He also identifies "a peculiar radio effect" in which a jazz band can be heard playing through his body when he stands in one spot on the concert stage. He admits that the "audience couldn't understand what was the matter with me, and I was afraid to tell them: they would of thought I was crazy. But I heard that jazz band playing" (194). In fact, one of the later manifestations was his identification of himself as "a human radio."[12]

Taylor Gordon died 5 May 1971, some twelve years after his final return to Montana from the East, but his decline had already begun in the late 1930s. Between 1940 and 1942, he became obsessed with proving that John Steinbeck had stolen *The Grapes of Wrath* from his unpublished novel, "Daonda," written during a stay in White Sulphur in the winter of 1935–36.[13] After 1947 Gordon's mental collapse initiated a cycle of institutionalizations that lasted until he left New York for White Sulphur in 1959.[14]

Born to Be, however, exists in a space that is at once the White Sulphur preserve of his youthful anticipation of outward movement and the Montana retreat from his world-weary, exhaustive travels. In its pages, Gordon sings the ever-shifting songs of an early twentieth-century generation whose safe anchor in the West never quite matched the excitement generated by the motion of the East.

NOTES

1. Robert Hemenway's introduction to the 1975 edition of *Born to Be* by the University of Washington Press presented the book to a new generation of readers whose curiosity about the Harlem Renaissance sparked a new wave of race-conscious books. Hemenway's primary research into the Gordon archives in Montana, and his patient attention to all the facets of Gordon's life, particularly to the period after his prominence as a singer, have made his essay not only an exemplary treatment of Gordon but an indispensable resource salvaging *Born to Be* from the status of a "lost" text.

2. The original edition of *Born to* Be was brought out by Covici, Friede Inc. in 1929, the same year that Alfred A. Knopf published Nella Larsen's *Passing* and Frederick A. Stokes, Jessie Fauset's *Plum Bun.*

3. *Born to Be* received attention in the two leading black magazines, *Opportunity* and *Crisis,* where it was reviewed by W. E. B. Du Bois; in the majority newpapers in New York, the *New York Herald Tribune* and the *New York Times Book Review;* and in respected journals such as the *Saturday Review* and *New Republic.* See Bruce Kellner, *The Harlem Renaissance: An Historical Dictionary for the Era* (Westport CT: Greenwood Press, 1984), for entries on Van Vechten (367–68) and Draper (103–4).

4. See Kellner, *The Harlem Renaissance,* on Covarrubias (83–84).

5. David Levering Lewis, *When Harlem Was in Vogue* (New York: Vintage, 1982), 212.

6. Arnold Rempersad, *The Life of Langston Hughes,* vol. 1, *1902–1941: I, Too, Sing America* (New York: Oxford University Press, 1986), 117.

7. Bruce Kellner, ed., *The Letters of Carl Van Vechten* (New Haven: Yale University Press, 1987), 83, 85.

8. Lewis, *When Harlem Was in Vogue,* 288–89.

9. Hemenway, Introduction, xxxiii–xxxv.

10. Taylor Gordon to Carl Van Vechten, 25 January 1932, in James Weldon Johnson Collection, Yale University, quoted in Hemenway, Introduction, xxxiv.

11. Marshall Berman, *All That Is Solid Melts into Air: The Experience of Modernity* (New York: Penguin, 1984), 288.

12. Hemenway quotes Gordon's manuscript, "To Whom It May Concern" (Last Will and Testament), 25 December 1968, in which he asks that his house become a museum "and employ at least ONE COLORED PERSON," to memorialize Gordon, "the first man to produce a human radio" (Hemenway, Introduction, xli). Taylor Gordon's will is included in the Gordon Papers of the Montana Historical Society.

13. Hemenway, Introduction, xxxv–xxxix.

14. Hemenway's introduction provides an authoritative biographical account of Gordon's last years in Montana. It is based on his interviews and correspondence with Gordon, members of his family, and friends in Helena and White Sulphur Springs, Montana, as well on his primary research in the archives of the Montana Historical Society and the Beinecke Rare Book and Manuscript Library, Yale University.

FOREWORD TO THE ORIGINAL EDITION

SOMETHING new has happened in this book. It is not too easy to explain what, but obviously something new has happened. I suspect that a new kind of personality has succeeded in expressing itself. It is a type of personality that many writers have tried to express—one of the earliest examples perhaps is Mark Twain's Jim in *Huckleberry Finn*—but no one has been entirely successful until Taylor Gordon somehow got himself on paper, lanky six-feet, falsetto voice, molasses laugh, and all the rest of him, including a brain that functions and an eye that can see. The result is probably a "human document" of the first order, to be studied by sociologists and Freudians for years to come. Fortunately, for you who have purchased *Born To Be*, it is something more than that: it is an extremely amusing book.

The pictures of the big-hipped sporting women of White Sulphur Springs, Montana, the account of the adventures of the Pullman porter and the chauffeur to John Ringling, and especially, perhaps, the descriptions of parties in the homes of the great, are about as good as anybody could make them. Very little is related in this volume about Taylor Gordon's career as a singer. Save for a few brief passages this side of his life is scarcely referred to. The emphasis, certainly, is placed on his career as a servant. I fancy a great many people who will read this book are going to find it rather disconcerting to discover just how much an intelligent servant can observe. They will be the more perturbed by the realization that Taylor Gordon has usually been fairly amiable in his report: constantly you suspect him of concealing the most monstrous facts. On the whole, it is just as well for these subjects that the man actually liked Big Maude, Mr. Ringling, and most of the others. I hesitate to imagine what Taylor Gordon would be capable of thinking about anyone he didn't like!

Mr. Gordon has written just as frankly about his own race. Indeed, it is probable that he has even been a little more frank in dealing with the Negro. Some of his criticism is doubtless justified; some of it has been made by others before him. All of it, I should think, may be read with interest, and possibly profit. It is a pleasure to be able to state that snobbery, racial or social, is lacking from this book. Big Maude, who ran the principal sporting house in White Sulphur Springs, Montana, traced her lineage back to the English nobility. When, many years later in London, Mr. Gordon was introduced to members of the English nobility, he immediately became aware that Big Maude had told the truth!

Anyone acquainted with the lyrics of the Blues will not be astonished to learn that one so unskilled in the art of belles-lettres as Taylor Gordon still writes with accurate observation and a poetic use of metaphor. Certain phrases in this book are unforgettable: "When I sing to people, ten thousand sing to me." Has ever the effect upon an artist of an audience, with its warring factors, been better expressed? Describing John Ringling concocting an omelet, he writes: "He could make an egg look like the froth on frozen milk.". How exactly he has set down the essential difference between American and French sporting crowds in the following sentence: "The people in Paris would empty the large grandstand like a fire drill in the public schools between the races." And there is a paragraph about Queen Mary that will make one forever weep for royalty.

Taylor Gordon has herein given his account of his first meeting with me. The date was October 3, 1925. I was interested from the first tone the boy produced, and Meda came out of the kitchen to listen—an excellent sign in the matter of Spirituals. The first song I heard him sing was *Done found my lost sheep*. I remember wondering at the time if he had ever really lost them.

CARL VAN VECHTEN.

New York, August 23, 1929

---

* Born To Be was on press at the time of the death of Geoffrey Scott, who is spoken of in this book.

INTRODUCTION TO THE ORIGINAL EDITION

By Muriel Draper

TAYLOR GORDON is a human being. He has written the story of his life as such. Birth, illness, growth, fear, gain, loss, God and the Devil, move in the flow of his living, each at its own pace, unified by the steady curiosity of a man who forever wants to know what he was born to be.

As life has come to him, so has he recorded it. Where it has confused and hurt him, baffled him into momentary blindness, so is it set down: where it has thrilled and amused him, the gaiety and excitement are clear to see. At times he has moved deeply with it into truth.

His style is his own, formed to carry his experience into written words. The very words themselves become his own. His utterance is as spontaneous as the circulation of blood in the human body, and subject to as many changes. One word will bring with it a sudden rush of memory, and the direction of the narrative swerves aside to give it room: there it is placed because it must be, after which he returns again into the main progression.

The varying significance of each person and event in his life can be perceived immediately by his descriptive vocabulary: with it he can build a background of elaborately ornamented and pompous elegance, and then suddenly throw against it, in a few swift words, a statement of breath-taking simplicity. This violence of contrast is a delight. Unfettered by literary self-consciousness, he has made laws of punctuation and spelling to suit himself. At first glance, this produces an effect that might be viewed as an erratic caprice, though but little careful attention is needed to discover its purpose. Both eye and ear are refreshed by the experiment.

Honesty, humor and complete freedom from vulgarity make it possible for him to write of the acts and conversations of his fellow men and women with rare candor and poignancy. An unusually developed power of observation is exercised as interestedly upon himself as upon those individuals and scenes that surround him, and bring a richness of detail and accuracy of awareness into use with startling effectiveness. Even when not interested, he is dutiful to the task in hand, telling the story of his life and asking the reason of it, and though the chronicle occasionally slackens, it never ceases to move.

Taylor Gordon is a Negro. His book is as free of racial self-consciousness as it is of literary self-consciousness. Being born into the only family of colored people that lived in a white community, he found himself soon and naturally at work. He worked for his own family, and gradually became almost desperately useful to others. He earned money and encountered adventure in so doing, and was grateful for both. His difference in color caused him no perplexity: he profited by it—a felicitous accident. These unique circumstances fortified him against the difficulties of his later life, and made it possible for him to meet them as the problems of a human being, the comic strengths and tragic weaknesses we share. He is surprised and sad and disturbed by unnatural misunderstandings, but fearlessly angry and critical when they are accepted in deliberate passivity. Ignoble as such things can be, they have not uprooted the gay pride that is deeply planted in his race.

* * *

The editing of this book has been pleasurably hazardous. The original manuscript is so complete a graph of the man himself that I was seriously tempted to photograph it and have it delivered into the hands of the reader, with every tone of voice and design of gesture thus clearly reproduced. Enfeebled as we are by the "fierce legibility" of type, this would have limited his audience to those of us who enjoy the effort of deciphering the code of another person's life. The book deserves a larger audience, so the delicate task of translating the crescendos and diminuendoes of his emotion and thought from his richly patterned page to the comparatively sober restraint of ordered rows of words in nice white spaces, was undertaken.

Enchanting quirks and sworls accented the vowels that sang in his ear. Crabbed little thick black marks indicated the consonants that choked in his throat. Where the meaning was to him obscure, small painful letters crept tightly around his words. As he wrote himself into bright understanding, the words were large, shapely things moving freely across his page. An orchestra of musicians, as yet unformed, might interpret this script more closely than a printing press.

To sever the man from his written words has occasionally seemed a cruel operation. I trust that I alone will feel it as such, and that the chanting of his diction and the beautifully scaled sound of his laughter may be heard as one reads; that the body entirely moving at the impetus of a thought and the eyes filled with stilled wetness at the impulse of a feeling, can be somehow seen through the words.

The book is exactly his. No word appears that he has not written or spoken. Naturally enough, congestion had to be relieved; snags occurred that it was desirable to clear away: but his diligence and intelligence made light of this. All questions were answered with such scrupulous verity that only time and the patience that all interest begets were needed to accomplish the work.

Often an event was so vivid and unforgettable to him that he ignored the fact that not everyone to whom he was relating it was there. Now and again, this caused an abrupt transition of scene that was uncomfortable, such as the sudden leap from the deck of a steamer to the streets of New York, a jump from the pantry of a Pullman car to the kitchen of a Broadway restaurant, an exit from a London drawing-room to a Harlem rent party, with no warning. Where the situation was supported by means of the underlying drama, this served to heighten it, but where it was merely a question of the mechanics of moving from one place to another, something had to be done about it. His procedure was simple. He would hold his head in his hands, shut his eyes, and say:

"Wait a minute . . . wait a minute. . . . Let me see. We got into dock at ten o'clock in the morning—no, it musta been about five in the afternoon, because I remember the sun was hanging kinda low. . . . No, no; I'm wrong: it was the morning. The sun wasn't hanging low, it was creeping high."

Few writers can handle the burden of time and place so simply. Yet it does not prevent him from distilling things seen, heard and felt in the alchemy of his own consciousness, and bringing them out at the right distance from the reader, to be viewed without the embarrassing intimacy that an obstinate fidelity to actuality imposes. So he achieves reality.

Matters of punctuation and spelling were not so simple, though here again, careful searching revealed definite plans. His mother is not always his Mother; she is sometimes the woman who gave him birth. His people are not unchangeably Negroes, or even Colored People: they are just negroes and colored people, along with white people, and french sofas; kings and queens are Kings and Queens. Strange tiny coronets floated above them in the manuscript. God and the Devil will so remain, buttressed by the stability of his belief in them, though gods and devils may abound.

Asking him why he wrote two words as two in certain parts of his story, but as one in others, such as "kinda", "anda", "musta", "ona", he answered, surely and quickly:

"Well—you see—if it's me talking, I use 'kinda' and 'ona', but if it's me talking about you talking, I use 'kind of' and 'on a'." . . . Perfectly good reason.

All his processes are so innately true that if falsity drifted carelessly into the structure he was building, it was ill at ease. It could be dispersed with the touch of a finger, though he would fight with superb tenacity of tooth and nail for the protection of what had been compounded out of the essence of his living experience, however blind I might be to its significance. Books should be written that way.

*   *   *

Taylor Gordon has given his readers his life as a human being, a man and a Negro.

It is a valuable gift.

BORN TO BE

There lived: A beaver-brown skin woman;
In a rickety shack.
With five kids, no husband, an'
Rickety furniture to support her back——
Amung a white settlement, on a
Fertile valley;
Away up in the heart-a-the Rocky Mountains:
They nick-named me Snowball.

CHAPTER 1

MY BEGINNING

THE first thing I can remember is my home. From there I will tell you of the trail I've mouched and the things a little black poor boy might experience on his trip through the great forest of delusion, canyons of bricks, wood and glass made by men.

(Do you think this life we live would be a miserable thing if each individual at the age of five knew every act and duty they were to perform before they reached the grave?)

First I'll tell you about my father and mother. That's far enough back to start with. Although they were not the beginning of me, they were the first ones to produce me here as hair, bones, flesh and blood.

I don't know just where my father was born. What little I know about him is hearsay, I being the only one in the family that never saw him. Mother said he was tall and straight with large eyes and pearly teeth that made his smooth black skin seem much darker than he really was.

He told mother that his forefathers were Zulus. His father went to England when a boy about eighteen, where he was employed as a domestic servant for a very wealthy Scotch family. They sailed to America bringing his father with them. At that time his father was twenty-

3

six years old. In America the Scotch family lost their money and sold everything they had, including his father. Then they returned to England. Somehow, after the Civil War, Grandfather and Father landed in Ohio, where my father went to a school of domestic science.

He got his papers as a first-class chef in Ohio. After school the family moved to Cairo, Illinois. In Cairo his father died. Soon after his father's death, he met mother, known as Miss Annie Goodlow of Licking River, Kentucky. A short courtship and they were married in Cairo. They only stayed there long enough to get their things together and move to Chicago. In Chicago he got a job as chef for a large gold-mining company whose headquarters were at Fort Benton, Montana.

Mother and Father were sent to Fort Benton. They stayed with the company until it sold out and moved its headquarters back to Chicago. The company wanted to take Mother and Father back with them, but Ma and Pa liked the free open country and decided to stay in Montana.

After going from camp to camp and town to town for years, they finally wandered into White Sulphur Springs, Montana. If God ever did spend any time here on earth, that must have been His hang-out, for every little thing that's natural and beautiful to live with is around White Sulphur.

Father was employed as a chef for the leading Hotel— The Higgins House—at that time a new three-story brick building with about a hundred rooms, stove heat, no running water, narrow front and back stairs, a small

4

office on the ground floor with windows facing north and west. On the east side, from front to back, they had a large dining room. Just back of it was a big kitchen taking up half of the south end of the building. On the southwest end they had a big saloon.

Father and Mother bought a shack in White Sulphur Springs that they called home. Father lived there until, about two months before I was born, he went to Canada to cook for a Canadian railroad—never to return. He was killed in a wreck.

I never did hear anything about his mother. My mother was born a slave on Pondexter's Plantation near Lexington, Kentucky. She didn't know anything of her parents. All she remembered about her childhood was just after her ninth birthday, at the outbreak of the Civil War. Her duty was to take the mistress's white saddle-horse up into the woods every day before sun-up, and keep him there all day long for fear the War Department would see him and confiscate him for the Army. (They robbed all the farms and stables in the district.) At dark she would return to the plantation, and then her mistress would ride in the dark with a black blanket that almost covered the white horse.

She used to tell me about the camp meetings in which she was one of the lead singers. My *Gawd!* what a voice she had! She was always singing while doing her work. On a summer's evening you could easily hear her singing a half mile off, voice just rising and falling, keeping time over a wash tub with the up and down movement of her body.

I was the last one of six kids to see the light—all boys but one sister, Anna, who didn't like that name and changed it to Rose Beatrice Gordon. We are all living but one, Arthur. He died from the whooping cough when he was one year old.

I was born between six and seven o'clock on Saturday morning, April 29th, 1893, at White Sulphur Springs, Montana, in a little three room shack with two gables, two doors, four windows and a cloth ceiling.

I can recollect the day my brother George and I were sitting on the back porch. I guess you can call it a porch —at least a stoop; there were two-by-fours laid on the ground, ten inch boards nailed on top of them, a canopy of boards that stuck out some eight feet. It was all walled up on the west side. The east side was open and a walk was laid of two boards, end-wise, to the chicken house built east of the shack. We each had a bowl of oatmeal and milk to eat, with bibs around our necks, just enjoying ourselves. It was one of those winter days in Montana that's like spring. They used to have them especially after a big snow storm, and the snow would melt, just right for snowballing. Who should happen to be passing but Orlow Danzer, being about fourteen then, and his little brother, Grover.

The sight of us sitting there on the porch was too much for Orlow, the oldest. He took a pot shot with a good solid snowball. It hit right in the center of George's porridge bowl. Well, you can never believe one bowl of oatmeal and milk could cover so much space. It whitewashed George for fair. Were it not for his mouth being

wide open hollering, you would have thought he was a snowman. It frightened me so, I couldn't holler at first. Ma came running out of the kitchen door just in time to see Orlow's and Grover's heels turning the corner of the Hill barn, about a block east of our back yard. She didn't know what had happened at first, George was kicking up so much noise; and by that time, I myself had joined in the chorus.

After mother found out that we were only frightened, and saw some of the snowball sticking on the inside of George's bowl, she laughed. She then told us the boys were only playing, and took us into the house, washed our faces and gave us clean bibs.

A little while later we were playing in the front room on the west side of the house. This was the room where we all gathered at night with Sis reading the news, Bob, my oldest brother, playing the violin, banjo, Duolyne harp, or some other musical instrument from Sears, Roebuck and Company. (He had a mania for all new musical instruments. The more freakish they were, the better he liked them. But his best holt was the fiddle that he managed to play good enough to earn money with, playing for dances.) With the exception of a bed, (Mother and sister slept in that room) a stove and a few chairs, we could hardly get into the place for musical instruments—piano, bass viol, horns—oh! I can't name them all. And drums too.

Bob also had a hobby for toy steam engines. He was quite clever. He made a couple that really ran when steamed up. George, who is five years older than me, lit the alcohol burner under one of these little steam engines. It was setting on the floor in the northeast corner of the room by the bass drum. Then we began playing with some other toys—fire engines and blocks. Soon this engine began to whiz, then it started to run. We stopped playing with the blocks, went to a contraption attached to the engine that sawed matchsticks on a little circle-saw which Bob had made out of a large clock wheel: it was run by a fish-line belt. It wasn't long before that became work, so we returned to the other toys without putting out the burner. In scarcely three minutes' time since we left the thing, it blew up. WHAM! it went. It busted the heads of the drums, cracked the bass fiddle, set fire to the carpet and wall paper, a piece of it flying across the room and breaking a looking-glass which was screwed to the wall on the south side of the room. It was a good thing there had been a chinook all day, causing the rain barrels outside of the front door to be full of melted snow water, or probably the house would have burned down.

Mother came running from her work again. The fast movement of her two hundred and forty pounds shook the whole house. She was wild. She had cautioned George before about playing with Bob's things. He got a licking of his life this day. I being the youngest, got away with a mean back-hand slap. George and I flew into the middle room under the bed where we slept. While under the bed, we could hear Ma talking to herself as she was straightening up the room—about how she didn't know what she was going to do all by herself with such bad boys. Then came a scream from her: "My God! You've broken the looking-glass! That means seven years' bad luck!"

You know, mother was very superstitious and took that evil omen seriously, so much so that she cried aloud like a baby. She closed the door between the middle room and the front room. Then she began to pray. She asked God for everything. The way she prayed, you'da thought she was talking to someone personally. At any rate, God must have been out, or else listening to some other adherent, more faithful than she. And when I think of her sincerity to Him, I can't understand why, if He is as generous as they claim Him to be, her path was piled so full of pitfalls, boulders and mountains.

Mother was right about the looking-glass *hoodoo*, I must say. We sure had seven years' hard luck. Every year we kids had some kind of contagious disease—whooping cough, measles, chicken pox, mumps, scarlet fever; then I broke my arm; next diphtheria, which was my hardest fight for life. About three months after I got up from diphtheria, I became paralyzed in my legs. That lasted six months more. Then from six years old until I was thirteen I had something new every spring; along about April or May, I would take down sick—the last kid in town that was going to have the latest pestilence.

Every Sunday the town ball-team would play ball up on a hill, just above our house on the southeast end of town. These teams were made up of clerks, teamsters, miners, bankers and gamblers. Many a Sunday, as I looked out the west window of our house at the gang

9

training up the hill to the game, some school kid would spy me there and deaden my soul by calling me a weakling. But by the latter part of June I was always good for a healthy run until the next spring.

I guess when I die it will be in the Spring.

Now, during my healthy periods, from my seventh year on, my duty began with running errands for Mother, like carrying in the wood at home or getting the mail for the lewd women that lived in the section below us on the east end of Main Street, south side, back of a twelve foot board fence, which Irkson had built because one of the girls called him one day as he passed riding his bicycle.

White Sulphur Springs is one of these Western towns built between two high hills in a valley surrounded by mountains. The highest peak, that forms the shelter on the west, is listed geographically as Mount Edith: Old Baldy, the natives call it, because of its snowy cap the year round. On the south, sixty miles away, you can see the Crazy; on the east, the Castles, named so because of their natural likeness to the architecture of the real castles of old Europe; on the north, the Clear Range runs around until it meets the Castles.

Over this range in the winter—January and February —at night come the flashes of the most beautiful Northern lights. It's nature's grand opera season. Ah! many a night have I had a beer-box seat in that valley while the Grand Mistress of Art displayed her greatest kinetopic plays. Mountain peaks for actors and actresses, the Aurora Borealis for background, while coyotes and wolves sang *a cappella* their weird harmonies.

About 1903 found the little burg at its height of success. All the mines were running double shift, Copper Ropelious being the nearest, and working about a thousand men. The valley was full of live-stock and plenty of help on every ranch. Eight good saloons and back of each saloon they had a gambling room. Every store and most every business place but the Postoffice had slot machines in them, but not the kind they have around here now-a-days. These were big machines, standing five and a half feet high, beautifully decorated like an Italian accordion, always a little cupid at the top center of the dial, to mark the amount won—if any. You put any coin in them from a nickel to a silver dollar. Puck, the best bet, paid forty for one. Frank Phelps had a whole batter of them and I have seen them all working at once.

There were many persons who came to White Sulphur Springs to bathe for their health. It is one of the best Springs in the world, with eighteen kinds of different minerals good for many things. Of all the sickness strangers brought into town, few of the populace died of it. Every once in a while, some oldtimer, over seventy, would peg out. But of all the kids that had all kinds of diseases, I can't remember but two dying while I was a kid, George Ford and Harold Anderson. Probably if their people had not had so much money, they would have pulled through too. They were not allowed to rough it like the rest of us boys, so they couldn't stand the gaff.

The City ordinance ran the main water-line through the center of the town from the head of Willow Creek. The reservoir is over a thousand feet above the burg in the Castle Mountains. (They don't need any fire engines there. You can shoot water onto the highest building in town through a three inch nozzle. There's so much pressure, they can't leave the head gates open. It would burst the pipes in the city.) That's as much as the city would do and anyone who wanted water on his own lot had to dig his own ditch and buy his own pipe. Everyone with money did. We were among those who didn't.

Mother used to take in washing, and on special occasions she cooked the suppers for the big balls held in the Auditorium. She also used to go out and cook for the best people in town—that is, the rich people— so she needed plenty of water. We kids had to keep the water barrels full, great big hogs-heads and whiskey barrels. We used coal-oil cans cut out at the tops—not all out, but just a three-inch V in the corners. Three tins would fit tight in a little express wagon they sold at Anderson, Spencer, Manger and Company. We hauled the water from the fire-house, a small two-room board building where the city kept the hand carts, two chemicals, and two hose. Just outside of the big doors, to the right, they had a large bell to be rung by whoever saw the fire first. The City Marshal also rang that bell every night at nine o'clock for the kids to clear the street, a law few paid any attention to.

The fire-house was three blocks north of our house.

It was a short cut to go through the tenderloin district, so naturally we kids fell to the job of supplying all the houses on the line on the south side of Main Street with water. None of these houses had water in them but the Blue House, so named because of its paint. There was a well built in the kitchen, but some of the girls didn't like that water to drink. Every evening we used to carry them a pail of drinking water.

George, being much older than I, gave me the air as a playmate, so I spent some time by myself until I met Dude Potter. Dude was his nickname. His real name is John V. Potter. His father was a short, fat man with silver-white hair, a round face and stiff, bowed right leg. He was shot on the kneecap during the Civil War. They had lots of money and a big sheep ranch on the Muscle-Shell, near Martinsdale, Montana. We got along fine for some time, but his scope was so small. If we were not on his saddle-horse, we had to confine our play to their large lawn and a back yard where they had a small garden, chickens and a stable. Then Dude's time was limited, too. He could never be out later than five, and he couldn't think of going on an errand with me for Lu LaMount or May Cooper, who might call at any time.

The girls seldom had to come for us kids. You can hear so far out there, all they had to do was raise a window or step outside the back door and holler, "You, *Man-n-n-n-neeee*", or *"Geor-r-r-r-geeee"*. They never called us by our nicknames, Jud, my brother's, or Snowball, a name I could never understand why they nailed to me, because it was George's bowl that was hit by a snowball that time. It followed me a long while, being succeeded by Zip, because I caught a hot fly off the bat while pitching ball to a high-school boy one day. (I never did tell the truth about that thing until now. When I pitched the ball, Bruno hit it so hard and drove it like lightning straight back at me, I threw out my gloved hand to protect myself, and the darned ball stuck in it like glue. My hand was numb for twenty minutes.) The lewd women only came to the house on special occasions when they had a note to be carried to someone they didn't want the other girls in the house to know about. Sometimes they came up for Mother to tell their fortune with cards or tea leaves. She earned lots of money at that. For a person who couldn't read or write until she was fifty—(we kids taught her)—she had a marvellous occult sense for that art. Many a blues she cured for the girls, and I mean they had 'em bad—on Mondays especially, when all they had earned during a good week-end's business their pimps would lose in gambling between four and eight o'clock Monday morning.

*　　*　　*

I started to school when I was six years old, at the White Sulphur Springs High School. It was a two-story building with eight rooms. They taught the kindergarten and the first grade on the same floor, boys and girls together in all classes. The kindergarten room was on the ground floor east side; the second and third, west; then fourth and fifth on the north end, and from the sixth grade to the graduating class on the top floor. My school days were filled with ups and down. I never made a whole season on account of sickness. Grammar I just couldn't get into my head. Although I studied it hard, I never passed an examination on it in my life. Drawing those houses and real estate plots, then putting the right adjective and conjunction in, is too much for me. But in History, Geography, Arithmetic and Physiology, I could read the book through and remember enough to pass the classes with high marks. I never could spell. Words never sound like they spelled them to me. I am sorry no one ever told me when I was at school, being that I didn't ask, just what good one would derive from study. The only thing I could figure it out to be for was to keep kids out of trouble. I could always find much more interesting things out of school; that's why I played hookey—to go fishing, hunting, or to the Caves, and sometimes to work on some contraption I was making.

I liked the games and running events, and the fights about the ground between the boys and the girls. They were always interesting as long as no one got badly hurt. I was always the only black boy in my room. Sis and George attended school at the same time I did, but they were far ahead of me. I went as high as the Eighth grade and quit. I looked like a giant among pygmies. Besides, I liked the outdoor life.

One day I was hunting brass and copper at the trash pile. We used to sell it to Herman Petzel, a German with no hands. They had been blown off by dynamite caps. But say! how he could write with those nubs. The best in town. He put the pen between them and pushed both arms. And fight! Many a guy he put out with a kick under the chin or a punch in the eye with a nub. Who should I meet at the trash pile looking for the same thing I was but Grover Danzer. He was just one year older than me. Grover had found bottles he couldn't sell because there was only one saloon in that town that would buy that kind of a bottle; he and his brother had been blackballed there on account of being accused of stealing bottles from the saloon-keeper's (Jim Monahan) own back yard. I had some which I couldn't sell for the same reason, but at another saloon, Bates and Wild. So we decided to go in partnership—junk and all. The deal made us close friends for years. He was an ideal pal. Run fast, good shot, perfect at snaring fish, and he kept his mouth shut about the errands. Also, any time was his time to be home. There were eighteen kids in the Danzer family, so one wasn't missed much.

We remained partners in all we could beg, borrow and steal until he quit school at the Seventh grade. Then his older brothers took him to his father's ranch. So that left me alone again, figuratively speaking.

I never was much for kids that couldn't do anything and most of the kids in town had many *can'ts* tied to them—their mother's and father's laws which they lived up to.

Not having any special pal, I played all over town; one day on the east side, the next day on the west side, and so on. I did all the errands for the girls in the cribs by myself for some time, busy from four in the afternoon until late at night. It was a good thing, I guess, for me to be cast alone, for my underground mail route was getting very complicated. Maybe Grover might have gotten wise too much, and by chance some day let the wrong word slip. I'da been ruined.

Human nature is surprising. Do you know, away out there even in those days, the girls' business associations and customers were not all miners and bachelors. I fitted right in the network perfectly on account of the pigment of my skin. I was accepted both high and low, never questioned why or what I was doing in conspicuous places. My alibi could be mother sending laundry home, or a city sheik sending a note to his sweetie, or Jim Omar, the meat market man, might be having me deliver some meat. I used to borrow his delivery wagon for sham in tight places. But generally my face was a passport stamped in full. I was even admitted into the saloons long before boys of my age were. Some of those people would turn over in their graves, if they are dead, if they could know what many of my movements were for.

CHAPTER 2

MOTHER'S FORESIGHT

MOTHER'S foresight gave me an early start. One
day Lawrence Dilworth, (the handsome young
man with white hair who clerked and drove Anderson,
Spencer and Manger's delivery wagon) had six of us kids
riding with him on a load of oats going from the ware-
house to the store. I got fresh and jumped off while the
wagon was moving, breaking my arm. That happened in
late summer. I was getting along fine when the first frost
came and I was quite sure I was over all my child ill-
nesses, as mother called them. I thought I had had everything possible people could have. But not so.

At this time a mulatto woman came to town as maid
for a family of sporting life people with two kids,
Archie and Edna Meek. The husband was a great poker
player. He could cheat with the cards—deal seconds,
set pat hands, all that stuff. He put out a couple of
cold decks. Then the gang of gamblers got wise to him.
He had to leave town first, then send for his wife.

The kids had the scarlet fever. Mother knew that if
anything like that was in town, George and I would
get it way late. Bob and Sis were never sick much, in
fact Bob couldn't take anything—even vaccination.
Mother carted George and me up to the Meeks' house
on the big hill, north side of town, and made us sleep

18

all night with these kids. Nine days later George began throwing up and crying of a sick headache. The next day we were both sick with scarlet fever.

I never knew a thing that I loved as I did orange juice, could become so boring. Doc McKay gave us orange juice in everything. I did not have the scarlet fever heavy, so most of the six weeks that we were quarantined I spent shooting strange cats that passed our back fence. I shot through a broken window pane. The hole was two inches long in the corner of the kitchen window. During the quarantined weeks George learned to play all the chords on the piano by himself. He has a fine musical ear. I was glad when they took the yellow sign off the house and I could go about my business—errands, water, bottles and junk.

Big Maude, a new landlady who came to town with four new girls, made me page and cash boy in her new house on the sporting line. Maude claimed to be of big English stock, some kind of Lords or Dukes, but because her people wanted her to marry some Knight, whom she didn't love, she ran away from home and decided to be a worldly woman to spite them. With her was a pretty little black-haired Irish girl who had a real brogue, and three American girls who claimed their families were rich too. But love drove them to prostitution. Maude had a real idea and mind for the business. She was the first to build an extra room especially for dancing on the old log house, put in a piano and redecorate the rooms. You could tell that Maude knew what a man wanted, although she claimed to be a green-horn at the business.

With her big-city air, dressed every night in swell gowns, making all the girls dress too, her house was the Palace on the line. In all the other cribs, the girls worked in gingham gowns, kimonas, Spanish shawls, semi-nudes, or a large ribbon tied around the bust with a hip sash hanging down on one side.

Before Maude came, a round of drinks cost a dollar anywhere on the line, no matter if you were alone or ten, a dollar right on. She raised it to five dollars.

Maude dressed me up in a blue suit with brass buttons. I was surely proud of that suit and my job, the only page in town. I was on duty from eight-thirty until one every night except Saturdays and Sundays. Later on, those nights. All the miners, farmers and city folks were out hitting it up on week-ends and the crowds lasted longer.

You'da died laughing if you'da been there one night. Old Billy Leapopa, a rich Scotch farmer and stock-man, always came in town on Saturday nights. He drove two fast trotting black horses hitched to a spring buggy. The big red barn was his put-up, a building with over two hundred stalls. Old Billy. Everyone called him by his first name, in fact the whole of Meagher County lived as one big family.

Well, Billy fell into Maude's half lit up, and ordered a drink for himself and the girls. This was around nine o'clock. Maude was the only one dressed for the evening. She told me to serve the drink while the girls were getting ready. I did. But when I asked for the five spot, Billy like to hada fit. He told Maude he had been buying drinks in whore-houses for twenty years and he knew what the price was. But Maude was his master. She sprung her high English on him, telling him she was ashamed of him as one from her land across the water. Old Billy became embarrassed and coughed up the five. He kinda laughed and told Maude that he had heard of her beautiful lasses and her wonderful self and he wanted to meet all.

Maude called for the girls to hurry dressing, like a dowager would shout to her guests when she called them to gather in the parlor to explain the rules of the game they were going to play. The words had hardly fallen from her lips when the door bell rang.

I opened the door. A lot of fellows fell in, most of them town boys who had been away to college from White Sulphur Springs. I won't call their names. They were a fast lot with plenty of noise. The piano player came in and began playing the *Midnight Fire Alarm*, his opening number. He called that his fast classic and masterpiece, although I think *A Hot Time in the Old Town* his best. He played that out of this world. The young fellows were too fast for Billy. He was kinda lame, having been shot in the leg for something—I never did learn for just what. So as fast as the girls would come in from their rooms, one of these collegiates would grab her and start dancing. After the dance he'd hold her for a chat. It looked like a bad night for Billy in Big Maude's Palace of Joy.

The stage coach was unusually late that night. The train was late at Dorsey. (That old Jawbone Road was never on time in the summer, so you can imagine what time it made in the winter.) I heard Butch Norse, the stage driver, whistle and crack his six horse whip. I'd know that whistle if I heard it in Purgatory. The custom was that as long as the mail came in before midnight it would be distributed, and the general delivery window would be opened. I told Maude the mail was in and asked permission to go for it. We had to be in the Postoffice when the window was opened, because after eight o'clock at night they never kept it open longer than when the last person had left the waiting room at that time.

Maude gave me permission to go. To get a letter at night, from the right person to the right girl, usually meant an extra two or four bits for me: from the wrong one to a girl not feeling too good meant a cussing out for me. They always laid the jinks on me as well as saying I was good luck. (Voluptuous moods.)

The next half hour I spent with the milling mob, jammed in the lobby of the Postoffice, talking, half whispering because the clerks couldn't work fast if the people made too much noise. At ten o'clock I got my bundle of mail. I knew every girl on the line by her real name and nickname. At times I ran for nearly fifty, steady, and more on off days, such as fast Saturdays and slow Monday evenings.

It was five blocks from the Postoffice to the first crib on the line, the Brown House. There were twelve girls in there at that time. I dropped their mail and hit on up the line—Blue House, the Cabins, then Bennett's place, the last and biggest house on the east end of the string, a big gray frame house with seven large rooms on the ground floor. I always saved Maude's mail until the last because I worked there steady.

There was a new girl at Bennett's, sent to her by some friend in Butte, without letting Bennett know that she was coming. The girl had just gotten off the stage coach. She still had her coat on. Her suitcase was setting in the parlor. Bennett's was all filled up. (Agnes Bennett was her name. Seldom anyone ever called her Agnes.) She asked me if I knew any house that needed a girl. I told her that Maude had an extra room, if she would take her. (Maude was so funny.) Bennett asked me to find out if Maude wanted the girl. I ran down the hill to Maude's and told her of the girl. Maude asked me what she looked like. Her house was full of men. I told her—five foot six, thirty-eight bust, blue eyes, chestnut hair, and young. Maude said, "My God! Yes! Get her quick!"

I went back to Bennett's, got the girl, her bag, and we hurried down to Maude's. I took her in the back door and called Maude to the kitchen. She gave the girl a surveying look from head to feet. Then they had a little chat. Drinks were selling too fast for Maude to have time to put over her fine points regarding her method on the business.

Jewell, that was her name, Jewell Hooks, was assigned to the Daisy Room. All the rooms in Maude's were named after flowers—Daisy, China Aster, Lily of the Valley, Tuberose, Rose Geranium, and over the maid's door she had Heliotrope. On Maude's door were large Orange Blossoms, painted by her own hands. Maude said she knew the language of the flowers and their interpretations expressed so much. Jewell was soon dressed and in the parlor, entertaining the guests *ad lib*. Old Billy fell for her, hook, line and sinker, and asked to be served in a private room with her. I took them one drink and had the time of my life again getting my five spot. I had to threaten him by saying that I'd tell Maude.

You know, a girl working for a name in Maude's was supposed to drink a drink every five minutes, or at least order them while on duty. Such a thing as bringing a bottle of whiskey of your own into any of the houses was a crime, but in Maude's it was murder in the first degree. Jewell, for whom Maude had chosen the right room, knew nothing about these rules. She was a novice of the first water. In the hands of old Billy Leapopa, a man nearly fifty with twenty years' experience in buncoing lewd women, Jewell was too soft for him.

At two o'clock, Maude called me to send me home, being an hour late. We checked up on my collections for the evening. Maude had a mind like an electric adding machine, started and stopped by a time clock: there was no way to fool her on her business. I counted out a hundred and eighteen dollars in her lap as she sat on the big low sofa, legs cocked and spread so that her dress pulled tight like a fireman's life-saving canvass.

When I said "a hundred and eighteen—that's all",

there came a funny sort of grin over her face and a grunt through her nose. *Humph!* Her lips tightened as her head turned kinda sidewise. Her eyebrows formed a high arch. Before a knowing smile came to her red face, she spoke. "You're holding out on me putty heavy tonight, aren't you?"

"Holding out?" I said. (Really I didn't know much about holding out at that time.) "No, that's all I collected."

"Who's laying down on the job tonight, then?" she asked.

You know, I hadn't learned to lie good yet, especially to Maude. She was hypnotic, so I told the truth. "No one," I answered.

"Did that new girl do any business tonight?" she inquired.

"Yes," I said.

"How much?" she questioned.

"One drink."

"One drink! My God! One drink in three hours! What kind of a house does that d— b— think I'm running?"

I was shocked pink. I had heard plenty of cussing before, but that was the first time I had heard Maude Healdyne cuss or even lose her city manners.

In a second she was on her feet. By the way, I have never seen such shapely feet on a woman of her height since. Nimble too. They carried a hundred and eighty pounds of violent woman down to the end of the hall into the Daisy Room without knocking in two jiffies. Old

Billy Leapopa had smuggled a quart of Kentucky Bourbon into the house. How? You'll never know, with Maude's eagle eyes on the watch. He and Jewell had drank most of it up. I heard Maude say, "And so, Miss Hooks, a bottle of Bourbon? That's why you have only called for one drink tonight, eh? Selling it yourself, what?" The girl was frightened stiff and didn't answer. Maude continued to talk in her high English tones. "Don't you know the rules of my house—that I don't allow any one to bring liquor in here? What do you think I'm running the business for?"

Jewell answered in a quivering voice, "I didn't bring the liquor in here. It's my first night to be employed as a useful companion for a gentleman and I don't quite understand it all. I heard it was not very thrilling work, although there was lots of money to be had for it, but so far both statements are wrong!"

Maude told her to put on her kimona and step out of the room as she wanted to talk to the gentleman. Her voice was so calm. Jewell had hardly gotten out of the door before Maude began playing the dozens with Billy. He tried to defend himself. The more she talked, the madder she got. She picked up Billy's clothes and threw 'em out the back door. The Daisy Room wasn't over six steps to the back door. Then she grabbed old Bill and yanked him out of the house, into the back lot. He was almost nude. Such cussing. My! oh my! You know, cussing coming unexpectedly and well rendered from some seemingly refined woman, is so effective. . . . She slammed the door after him and bolted it.

Jewell had gone into the parlor. She was lying on the sofa, crying like a whipped child. Maude came in and read the riot act to her. She told her all the fine points of the business in order to be successful. I thought she might turn on me with a slap for not telling her before that they were not drinking in the Daisy Room, so I slipped out the front door.

In order to get home quickly I started around the west corner of the house and turned south through the back lot. Old Billy Leapopa was trying to find his clothes in the dark on a half muddy ground. He heard someone coming and hollered, "Hey there, friend," rolling the r's laboriously, "help me find me clothes."

In those days I had eyes like an owl. In a few minutes he was dressed, but dirty for fair. He had stepped on some of his clothes and he put on his shoes without socks, after stumbling around in the muck ever since he had been outside. He handed me a bill. When I got home I found it was a twenty.

The next morning I had almost thirty dollars. I gave mother the twenty and she questioned me as to how I came by it. It was hard to make her believe the tale about Maude's acting. At any rate, she kept the twenty but told me I was getting too big to work around the girls, and that I should stop. I swelled up and began to pout. Ma threatened to whip me within an inch of my life if I didn't dry up. I knew she really carried out her words, so I sulked out of the house. At the end of the week, I quit Maude's. She gave me a new suit of clothes, a pair of shoes, a hat and a hand-painted picture of flowers—white pinks, canary grass laurel for good service.

I must look that combination up in Webster's dictionary some time, and see just what she had in mind.

CHAPTER 3

A TIN HORN GAMBLER DRIFTS TO TOWN

IT'S a bum poker player that just can't lay a full house down.

It was Frank Phelps, the King of Saloon Keepers, who built the bowling-alley alongside of the old Higgins House. He had bought this house some time before. They made him manager of two hotels and two of the best bar rooms in town. He was a man five feet, eight inches tall, with a large, well-formed head like William McKinley's, with mixed gray hair. He weighed two hundred and twenty pounds, and was one of the best poker and billiard players in town. Frank was known to kill more ducks with a double barrelled shot gun than any man in the State and he personally told me one time that he had drank enough good whiskey to float a battle ship.

In the day time it was easy enough to get boys to set pins, but after nine at night most of the goody-goody boys were home or forbidden to do that kind of dangerous work, so Grover and I fell heir to the night work at five cents a game. We were doing fine on the level, when a tin-horn Gambler blew into town with a big sorrel race horse. He came overland by saddle-horse from Lewistown, leading this racer. It seemed that he had been beating all the country fairs and private races in the eastern part of the state. Someone told him that the sheriff of Meagher County had a little guilden that he thought could run, and if he got to White Sulphur Springs, he could beat the county's pride easily and clean the town of all its jack.

Sparks (that was the Gambler's name) laid low for four or five days. He played poker, a little bowling, not gambling heavy. He was busy asking fly questions so that he could get the inside dope on the Sheriff's racer, Dixie, a black four year old with two white front stocking feet, a small star in his forehead, a swell little sprinter for a quarter mile, and weighing around a thousand pounds. Sparks wasn't much of a bowler, but there was much money to be won in the town's new game, so he tried to get us to bunch the pins for him. Grover was afraid of me, and I was afraid of him on that deal, because both of our older brothers played in the games. Besides, we knew if we were caught, men in the game wouldn't have thought anything of taking a shot at us. Most all the players carried guns of some kind, pearl handled ones, jewelled—anything from a vest pocket pistol to a thirty-two special, set on a forty-five frame.

Sparks used to hand us a dollar or something every time he met us on the street. All through the week at day time until five o'clock in the evening, there wasn't much bowling because men didn't like to set pins. But all day Saturday and Sunday until early Monday morning, loafted balls and falling pins could be heard for blocks. The town gamblers gave Sparks samhill on every game he played.

Finally his time came for the big race. H
up good. The majority of the betting peo,
backed Dixie. They ran the race up in Linc
just outside of the city limits, at the east end
a half mile race. The big sorrel beat Dixie
lengths. Sparks pretty near broke every gamble
and he would have left town, but his horse
think of his name) broke a blood vessel in l
during the race, and could not travel.

That night they had big bowling games. The
Sparks until the wee hours of the morning. The
day they beat him down at Mat Murphy's in l
By the end of the week, he was pretty badly bent
and his horse was still sick and couldn't travel. So Sp
made up his mind that the only way he could get e
was to get us to bunch the pins. At noontime whei
came home from school for lunch (for in those days
all went to school at nine in the morning, recess at te
thirty for fifteen minutes, home at twelve, back to schoc
at one, and out again at four) Sparks was sitting in the
kitchen talking to Mother. She gave us kids our lunch
of fried mountain trout with potatoes, bread and tea.
(Ma was a great tea drinker. We seldom had coffee—
even for breakfast we had tea.) Sparks did not have
much to say to me while we ate—Sis, George and I.
Bob and Sam didn't go to school then. Bob had graduated and Sam got cowboy-crazy and quit.

I finished eating first, grabbed my cap and ran out the
kitchen door. Just as I got through the gate, Sparks
called me. I stopped and he came to me. "You's gotta

bunch those pins tonight, or by God! I'll kill yah," he said. At the same time he slapped a ten dollar bill in my hand. I took the bill and ran, never answering him. On the way to school, I stopped in Heartfield's drug store on Main Street, bought a dozen delicious candy cakes they used to sell for a nickle, which we kids used to vamp the girls in school with and sugar the teachers. I always fell in love with my teachers then. Grover and I had more spending money than any of the kids in school, and were the raggediest.

I asked him to run down to the Springs with me. The Sulphur Springs are about a quarter of a mile from the school house. I told him Sparks gave me a ten dollar bill and what he said. But I wouldn't bunch the pins unless he did too. After school, Grover met Sparks at the corner of the Bank on Main Street. Sparks told Grover what he told me at noon, but Grover was wiser than I was. He told Sparks he would for twenty dollars and Sparks gave it to him. Grover could run like the wind. He tore out for home, me after him.

I couldn't catch him so I went home too, did my chores and errands, had supper, then went to the bowling-alley. They were having a double four-handed game at fifty dollars a man, playing fast, making good scores, averaging over two hundred a man. Sparks was playing on one of the teams, losing again. In fact, I think Hank, Skinny and Dr. Burnett were throwing off on him.

Hank was a good bowler, good for two hundred and twenty regularly when he rolled from the right hand corner. He had a wicked curve that took ten feet from

the head pin and swept the alley clean. Also he could roll a straight ball right down the center of the alley. He was using that shot and getting split after split. Sparks was sweating like a bull and losing his money.

At nine o'clock Grover and I took the pits. In a few minutes we began to set them in. Sparks said he was a thousand dollars loser at that time for the evening, with his side bets. By eleven forty-five, he was even and winner, betting doubling up. At one o'clock, they started an argument about the foul line. It lasted fully thirty minutes. The game continued. Soon someone spied that the pins were bunched and hollered, "Get out of there, you little bastards." We knew the time was up so we flew out the back windows. Just as we got out two shots rang out—*Bow Bow*—we could hear the bullets whiz after they had passed through the board wall. Our feet took wings.

I didn't see Grover any more until Monday at school. Neither of us returned to the alleys until Sparks left town. For three or four weeks after we were shot at, we spent our time at evenings in the office of the big red Sherman barn or the gymnasium, and sometimes at the Heartfield drug store. But seldom could we be in any of those places later than nine o'clock. The bosses always chased us out at that time, no matter how interesting the sheepherder's or stranger's tales might be.

One night we went into the gym, and just as soon as we poked our head into the door, Cleaber Tipton, the founder and Boss said, "You kids can stay in here if you fill up the wood-box and the watertank and keep quiet—and don't run all over the place!" They used wood to heat the water for the shower-bath. We accepted his agreement.

After the work was done, Cleaber came out of the dressing-room in his trunks. About fifteen or twenty men were in there, boxing, pulling weights and doing trapeze stunts. Mort Hate was trying to do the giant swing. He would get almost over the bar and fall back. Cleaber hollered at him, "Aw, come down and let me show you how to do that!" Mort dropped down and Cleaber took a running jump at the bar, about twelve feet high. He caught ahold of it and began to swing. After two attempts he began to do the giant swing. His hands slipped and he landed with his head under the stove, fifteen feet from the bar. How he didn't break his neck, no one knows, but Grover and I laughed aloud. He got up and kicked us out, and told us never to come back in there again if we couldn't keep quiet.

Our next hangout was with the Chinese.

CHAPTER 4

CHINESE NEW YEARS

THE Chinamen were having a big time in their wash-house on Main Street—lots of special dishes of food and drink were set on the floor and low tables for the occasion. Grover and I found lots of amusement with them, although most of their conversation we could not understand.

Once in a while, when one chink acted as if he were going mad in his debate with his fellow-men, we would ask Charley the Chinaman (the Boss of the laundry) what was the matter with him. We were surprised to learn that he was putting up all the fuss about some girl stealing his hop-pipe in Helena "long times ago," as Charley said, during a New Year's celebration, and every New Year since, when he got half drunk, he would argue the point that some day he would find her and kill her. His wrath impressed us that hop must be a grand thing, and a special pipe must have meant more than anything else in the world to a smoker.

From the Main Street festivities the chinks would visit down at Louie the Chinaman's place. He lived in a log cabin on the northwest corner of town. He owned a big truck-garden, kept plenty of hogs, and in his cabin he had ten hop-bunks. Grover and I would fall in line with the Chinamen as they strung out of the wash-house and wound their snakey trail down to Louie's, a mile away.

It was amazing how many people could get into Louie's cabin—one big room with small bunks all round the walls, two and three deep. Chinamen were playing dominoes, cards, and eating continually. A white woman here and there would be laying in a bunk—sound asleep or smoking a long hop-pipe. Her mouth seemed to be hardly big enough to gobble the big mouth piece. The stem of a hop-pipe is one inch in diameter. Every time I see a policeman's billy, I think of a hop-pipe.

White men sometimes gambled with the chinks, but most of them went to Louie's to smoke. It kept Louie very busy, getting up from his private bunk to get a paper of opium for a customer. He sold a little ladle-full from the small jars at a dollar a paper, as he called it—but it really should have been called tins. He had a hundred or more little round tins cut from tomato cans smoothed down, on which he put this opium. A dollar's worth would make three or four good pills. It's a funny thing about smoking hop. Most anyone can smoke, but few can cook it good, so that a nice round pill will stick to the pipe bowl without plugging up the little hole through which the smoke goes. Louie taught us to take care of the pipes and sell the opium.

Every night after dinner we were on the job until a married man of class came down too often and stayed too late. His wife put the Sheriff on Louie and he was run out of town; that necessarily cut our graft again. We used to steal the Yen Shee from the pipes and make a brown powder out of it and sell it to the cocaine fiends on the line. It gave them something of the same feeling as cocaine. Some snuffed it and a couple put it in whiskey and drank it. I would like to tell of other things that happened in Louie's den, but some fools reading about it might want to try them. If they didn't do it just right, they would wake up—maybe, and maybe not.

CHAPTER 5

WOULD BE MAN

BY the time Louie was closed down, my scope for runs was getting larger and larger. My speed on foot was faster, lungs stronger, voice louder. I was initiated into the gang of older boys, being tall for my age, although all the boys were older than I was.

Stray Goose was then their favorite game. It started some nights about nine o'clock and lasted until twelve or one. Maybe you don't know about Stray Goose. I'll tell you how it was played. The one who was to be the stray goose was the kid who won the block dash, no matter what block they were standing in at the time they decided to play. The race began from a gang-standing start. They all ran the block. The winner was given a half-mile head start on a straightaway. He must turn, holler "Stray Goose!" and then it was up to the mob to catch him. Every time he turned, he had to holler "Stray Goose." If they caught him, they could do anything they wanted to him except perform an operation or kill him.

One night just after a chivaree, they almost killed John Kerby. John was stray goose. The gang was standing in front of the big red barn. John walked down to the Bank Building and hollered "*Stray Goose!*" (It's a funny thing out there. You can hear a person holler a mile, and in the summer time, up in the mountains, the echo of your voice comes rolling back to you like three people answering you. If you holler, *"Yewhoooooo,"* then wait a moment, you hear *"Yewhoooooo"* almost as loud as you hollered it; then ten seconds after that it comes a little softer; and maybe twenty seconds later, when you think it's all gone, here it comes back to you very faintly—*"Yewhooooooo."* It's too marvelous!) The gang took out after John. He led them south three miles to the Pest House, east back of the graveyard, north through the trash pile, across town and was half way up Meek's Hill when Joe Matthews caught him.

John put up a fight. In the scrap Joe was banged on the nose. By the time the rest of us got on the spot, Joe was bleeding like a stuck hog. He told the gang what happened. Any time they caught a goose, they made a noise like a pack of fox hounds, and kids living near by would get out of bed to help torture the bird if they were not goodie mother's boys. They didn't always catch the goose. Many a time the boys turned back, tongues hanging out.

This night they didn't know what to do with John for putting up a fight. The gang decided to hogtie him and leave him sleep in Jim Stutteraw's hay loft nearby. He was tied and carried to the barn, but the place was locked. While the mob was planning something else, some kid backed Stutteraw's cart out from under the rain shed, with the suggestion to give John a ride down the back of Meek's Hill in the cart, coasting backwards. You know a mob never thinks. Before you could say jack robinson, John was piled into the footrack and turned loose down the hill, lined with buffalo trails. It looked like a huge staircase. The back of Meek's Hill was a forty degree slope all the way to the creek. That cart turned, twisted and bounced every way but upside down. John screamed like a madman. Most of the kids realized what they had done and hauled their hinies for home, leaving eight or ten of us there to see what would happen. With a little snow on the ground in spots, and the bright moonlight, every move of the cart was distinct. It bounded from fifteen to twenty feet at a time, jumping Omar's Irrigating Ditch, landing in Smith River, where it rolled across and buried the wheels in three feet of mud of the opposite bank. It was a good thing the water was low and the cart didn't turn a little east to Jim Omar's ice pond, with twelve feet of water in it. We all ran down to John, and pulled him out. He was cured and so were we. That put the end to Stray Goose for some time.

*　　*　　*

Spring brought me diphtheria and nearly put me out. I never knew one could hear and see so many strange things. If I could write the music down on paper that I heard while I was sick, I would not have much worry about finance. It was most beautiful, and sometime I shall try to paint from memory some of the animals that I saw.

Next came my period of paralysis. A queer thing, indeed! No pain. Just couldn't handle my legs. They went every way but the way I wanted them to go. I would leave home at noon and make it to Sherman's by one with my crutches—a half mile away.

Mr. and Mrs. C. H. Sherman are the finest people you ever met. Mrs. Sherman is from some of the old New York stock that moved to Montana when she was a little girl—her mother and father, three sisters and a brother—the Collins family. Her parents lived close to the hundred year mark, and the rest of them are going strong. Sarah was the best lady side-saddle rider in the state. She stuck bucking bronchos that cow punchers couldn't ride straddled with locked spurs. She is one lady that went West that never allowed her skin to turn to a burnished rough red like most of them acquire through carelessness. Her complexion is like a baby's until this day.

One day when I wasn't giving myself a thought about getting well, for to me paralysis was like all other things I had had which lasted for a while and passed on itself, Mrs. C. H. told me of an osteopath who came to town and who cured kids of paralysis after diphtheria. She gave me two dollars and sent me to him. I dragged myself over to where he lived, two blocks from her house. He laid me on a table, ran his two thumbs up my backbone, which popped like a brass thimble pulled over a wash-board. Then he made my legs go back to nearly touch my head. He half pulled my arms out, twisted my neck and made me get up. I broke out in a light sweat. My legs felt warmer. I took two more treatments and threw the crutches away in three weeks' time.

I have only been sick in bed once since then, and that's been twenty years ago. (Knocking wood.)

When my pins got good again, I had reached the point in life where all boys wanted to be men. I acted as much so as possible. I got high-heeled boots, a six-horse-roll on my pants, leather cuffs, Stetson hat, with a package of Bull Durham tobacco in my breast pocket and let the tag hang out, always chewing a match in company. I used to rig myself out this way for a dance. Nearly every week the people in and around Smith River Valley had a dance. These dances were held in the country or in White Sulphur Springs. On the farms, they usually danced in the hay mows. In the burg, they usually had their dances at the Auditorium, at two dollars a couple. The supper was a dollar a couple extra. They didn't sell whiskey at the dance hall, but plenty of it would be brought there and along about three o'clock in the morning the best dancers would be just tight enough to feel egotistic about their ability. As they were of all nationalities, Swedes, German, Scotch, Dutch, French, English and a few Roumanians, you can imagine the twist given to the American waltz and two-step, schottish and quadrille. Johnny and Mary Logan, who lived on a farm twenty miles from town, were the best in the country at the heel-and-toe schottish. If Johnny couldn't get some couple to challenge him before the night was over, he would get into a fight. He just must be in something prominent.

*   *   *

C. H. Sherman. I don't know what his blood line is. To me, he is a hundred percent Yankee. He owns one of the largest farms in the county and wintered hundreds of heads of cattle and horses in his hay field two miles north of White Sulphur Springs. I was seen so much with him on some of his saddle-horses, people thought I was one of his adopted sons. He taught me riding, driving, branding, dehorning cattle and putting up hay. He knew a lot of cowboy songs and many a tale of the wild and wooly West.

The first pay I got for a farm job from him was for driving the derrick during the haying season. He used the boom-pole derrick with nuts. I drove two big farm horses hitched to a mowing-machine cart. In lifting the hay to the stack, I drove from fifteen to a hundred feet straight away, then backed the team up. The higher the stack got, the farther out I would have to drive. I spent two seasons on the derrick job, then I ran the hay-rake for two seasons. I had two first class trotting cayuses, one bay and one black. One day Skinny Kinyon, a young fellow that handled the nets, told me that I would be able to make straighter windrows if I took a chew of tobacco; not that I was doing bad, but I naturally wanted to be a man, and chew on the job. Star or Plug Cut were their favorite brands. I took a chew, and began bouncing along on the rake. I swallowed some of the juice, and you have never seen a sicker boy than I was for an hour or so.

The next season I ran the Bull-rake. There is only one or two points higher in the haying business, and that was mowing and stacking hay. Shorty Kearns had the job of mowing for years, and I was in hopes that he would quit one season, but he didn't; so I lost the thrill of having that job, but I drove the mower one day while he was grinding some sickles. The highest salary I drew in the haying was two dollars a day.

Next I got so I could stick a cow-horse. A good cow-horse is hard to ride. He can run fast, stop short and turn quick. When I accomplished that, I joined the spring drive to Sheep Creek, the summer range for their cattle, and I always helped to bring 'em back in the fall, even after I became a chauffeur and only rode a horse on rare occasions. In all my riding, I have only been thrown from a horse three times—twice from tame horses that just got tired of carrying their loads and began bucking unexpectedly, and one time when a fellow from Two Dot, Montana, sold C. H. Sherman two black trotting horses with bald faces, harness, buggy and all. He told C. H. they were saddle-broke too. One evening, C. H. put a saddle on one, and he stood as still as an old milk cow. I thought C. H. was going to ride him. Instead, he told me to give him a little exercise. The horse never moved until I got on. Then he began bucking, in the old saw-buck fashion. He threw me straight up in the air so high that Powell Black, the town district attorney living on Knob Hill, could see me over the barn from his house. I came down feet first without a scratch. Black was from Kentucky, and he had a real Southern belly laugh. We could hear him in Sherman's corral, and it is at least a half a mile from Black's house, where he was sitting on the porch at the time.

It was with C. H. that I missed a chance of my life to get big money. One night the haying crew was laying around the cabin on Sheep Creek after supper. The card game broke up and they began telling lies. Finally they chose me to tease about being afraid of the dead, so to prove it, C. H. Sherman offered me ten head of young heifers and a bull if I'd go down to the canyon to the Old Breeds grave, inside of a little fence, and put a white flour sack on the cross that marked it. My brothers had told me so much about ghosts and Mother was so superstitious I wouldn't go. What I know about the dead now! It makes me sigh to think of that deal. They bluffed me and laughed themselves to sleep.

But I got even with C. H. one night. He and I were going to town from Sheep Creek in a Deadax wagon, loaded with a boom-pole for the derrick. We had Tom and Jerry in the harness. Tom was a beauty, a tall dapple sorrel with a thick bowed neck and white stocking feet. Jerry was a twin mate with the exception of a large bald face. They were two horses that surely knew when they were on exhibition. On a country road, they'd trot fast but there wasn't any particular style about their carriage. Just as soon as they saw a farm or another team coming, up went their heads, out went their tails and my! how they would step!—like dancing circus horses.

C. H. Sherman had been singing all afternoon and telling me tales. In a manner, he had said he wasn't afraid of anything, then brought up the Breeds grave again to me. Dark came on when we were twelve miles from town—just above the Dogy Ranch. Sheep Creek is thirty miles north of White Sulphur Springs. A big black cloud gathered in the west, stars disappeared gradually, sheet lightning could be seen flashing back of the hills. A fine rain started, then quite big drops came, spattering here and there. Soon it was hailing hail-stones as big as plums. Every once in a while one would hit Tom too far back, and he tried to run away. We never used a whip with that team—even for style. A bolt of lightning hit a tree not quite a quarter of a mile ahead of us and set it on fire. The clap of thunder was so loud that it deafened us so that we could not hear each other talk for a few seconds. Lightning played all around us. How we didn't get killed is a mystery. C. H. shut up and didn't say another word until we were unhitching in the barn in town.

We went to his house. His wife, Sarah, fixed a nice, juicy steak, stewed French peas, with hash browned potatoes, tomatoes, tea. She surely can cook! After dinner we sat in the parlor. C. H. got his pipe, pulled the Morris chair up under the reading light, made himself comfortable. Hell got into me and I told his wife what had happened—how he shut up like a clam out of water in the lightning storm. It was my laugh. He never could spring the Breeds grave on me without me hitting back with the lightning storm, so both jokes petered out.

C. H. Sherman was also Sheriff at that time, but he didn't live at the jail. All kinds of prisoners were brought to Meagher County jail and held until the Court session opened.

A fellow named Herbert H. Metzger killed a rancher by the name of Homer Ward, on Sheep Creek. He shot him through a window at night and robbed him. The law caught Metzger a month later and brought him to White Sulphur Springs. A bunch of us boys would go over to the jail from school and talk to Metzger through the barred windows from the street. He was very interesting. He had been in the Spanish-American War; travelled all over; and with the truth he knew and the lies he told, he always kept us coming back for more.

One day we went over to the jail. Who was in the cell next to Metzger but a crazy woman from Martinsdale, a cook from a sheep ranch. She was one of these insane people who talked incessantly about how her Boss had robbed her out of all her money—thousands of dollars. She used to swear once in a while, but most of her language was respectable. Metzger's stories from that time on were always spoiled for just when he would get to some tragic point, the crazy woman would put in some funny remark.

Mrs. Sherman felt sorry for the poor lady. She used to cook her dainties and send them to the jail by her husband. One evening the crazy woman got the idea that the under-sheriff was trying to poison her. She wouldn't eat anything more from him. So, Mr. C. H., the sheriff, had to go up to the jail and feed her.

It was on a Friday night that his wife and I went up with him in the buggy, driving Jerry single. Mrs. C. H. went in the cell room to talk to the crazy woman while her hubby was in the kitchen fixing the tray of food for her. The woman's talk with Mrs. Sherman was remarkably sane. Mrs. C. H. came out to the kitchen elated over the lady's improvement. Mr. C. H. took the tray of food into the cell while we all remained in the kitchen.

In a few moments there came a cry from the crazy woman. At the top of her voice she shouted: "Take him out! The Beast! Take him out! He tried to rape me! He tried to rape me!"

We all ran into the cell room. The sheriff was standing with the tray in his hands, from which a few things had been eaten. But married women are hard to convince. You can imagine the effect that had on the wife, especially just after her sane conversation with the crazy woman. It even made Metzger laugh.

The best joke the crazy woman put over on Metzger was when he tried to tell us about a gallant deed he performed during a hot fight in the Spanish-American War. It seemed his company had been ambushed somewhere in Cuba and their fate would have been the same that Custer and his troops met with, if it hadn't have been for him. He was living the battle over again. His black eyes flashed and his dramatic baritone voice held each kid rigid like a diamond dick novel. Just before he got to the climax he said, "Men were falling all around me. The grape shot was spatting the trees and peppering the ground. I stood like a man of destiny in the thickest of the fray. Why I wasn't killed was because the Gods of Heaven Themselves were protecting me. The Captain and his first lieutenant fell shot dead before me. I, being second lieutenant at the time, automatically took charge of the Company. Quick action was necessary to save our hides. What do you think my first command was?"

48

"Run like Hell," the crazy woman shouted in a high soprano voice.

We kids burst out into laughing, Metzger got raving mad and tried to shut the crazy woman up. The more she talked the smarter she got, and the louder we laughed. We never did learn what Metzger's first command was; at any rate it saved his hide. For a long time after that the kids' bywords were "What do you think my first command was?" Some other kid would answer back "Run like Hell."

The day they hung Metzger, the boys that liked him went fishing. We didn't care to be in town when they killed him, even if he was a murderer. He surely could entertain us.

*   *   *

Soon after that, I learned automechanics from Barney Spencer. He taught me how to dissect a car, put it in a tub of gasoline, pick out the parts, put them together and make the darn thing run.

Barney Spencer is one of the sons of the great old Al Spencer who helped to settle White Sulphur Springs, Montana, with Jim Brewer and B. R. Sherman and others. Old Al Spencer had three sons and two daughters. They were some of the richest people in town. G. K. Spencer is still a banker in White Sulphur Springs. Barney is still a great mechanic, although he doesn't need to be one. He has a couple of college diplomas for other professions.

He and I would sit up into the wee hours in the

morning, working on someone's car or his own. His kind
mother used to come and bring us all sorts of dainty
things to eat, but we couldn't have them until we cleaned
up our hands so that you couldn't have seen any of the
black grease on them, even under the finger nails. With
her insistence and Barney's patience, I learned to work
on an automobile and still have what she called dinner
hands.

After I learned to drive a car, I drove for pleasure for
some time—maybe Barney's or Dick Manger's or John
Potter's old Rambler. Then the Maytag company sent an
agent into the valley with "the car of the century," a
two-lunged drive, two-seated bus. Their great selling
point was that it could not get stuck on a hill. They had
the gas tank above the engine. They stuck many a
farmer on that bunch of junk. Cliff Tipton bought one
and put it on the road for passengers between Dorsey
and White Sulphur Springs, twenty miles away. (The
train hadn't gotten into White Sulphur Springs yet.) I
drove it too. He paid me sixty dollars a month. One
night I had some sparkplug trouble and it was eleven
o'clock that night before I got both cylinders hitting.
And to make sure before I went to bed I took a little spin
down the road. They used carbide lights on cars then.
Just as I crossed Smith River, a cow jumped up from
where she was laying and started to cross the road in
front of me. I put on the brakes and curved. The car
slid sideways and hit the cow flat on the ribs. It knocked
her down, but didn't damage the car. That taught me
about cows' attitude toward automobiles.

I made a month or two with Tipton, and though he was making money hand over fist, that wasn't enough for him. He wanted me to drive day and night. One morning I didn't get up at five o'clock to make an extra run for him, so he took the car and burned the crankshaft bearing out, and I quit.

Life was beginning to lose all of its thrill to me in White Sulphur Springs. I knew everybody by their whole names, nicknames and businesses, as well as by their habits. I knew all the ranches, mountain trails, hunting grounds, fishing holes, vacant mines and beautiful caves. Lots of people were leaving Meagher County—why shouldn't I? I ran away to Helena, Montana, a city of 12,000 then, for a short stay.

In Helena, I stopped at the Walton Hotel, a little two-story brick building at the head of Main Street. A high-brown skinned man was the proprietor, but his guests were both white and black. Helena had quite a few colored people scattered about the city, working at different occupations. The city was making ready for the State Fair to start in three days. All the decorated windows and lamp posts reminded me of the Fourth of July at home, only on a bigger scale.

I met a brown-skinned man named Jayson, who had been a soldier in the Philippines. He had a long saber scar on the left side of his head. At that time he drove Tom Crews' car. Crews was one of Montana's prospectors that had struck it rich. He walked into Helena from his claim forty miles east with his first strike of $17,000 worth of gold-dust in his pack. He was afraid to ride in the stage coach, fearing that it would be held up. With that money, he grew to be one of the richest men in the state of Montana.

Jayson and I were buddies because we were both mechanics, and our thoughts ran close together. With Jayson I saw lots of the country west of Helena. When I was alone, I visited all of the buildings in the city, the Capitol, Assay Office and Library. A couple of nights, I went out to Broadwater swimming pool, a short trolley ride west of Helena. Broadwater is something like a young Coney Island. Hundreds of people swim there nightly, a sport I always enjoyed ever since my big brother, Bob, threw me into Big Eddie, our swimming hole in White Sulphur Springs, just outside of town on the west end of Main Street. He made me scramble out all alone. Big Eddie was nine feet deep and had a fast current, but all the kids in White Sulphur Springs learned to swim there—never no bathing suits.

The fair started, and I went out to the Fair Grounds daily. After seeing all of the live stock and farm exhibits on the first day, I spent the other three days at the race track. I had my pockets picked for the first, and only time in my life—so far—on the second day at the track. Jayson was with me that day, but I lost him in the mob. It was ten minutes before I got out of the jam of people, rushing to the betting polls like a pack of hunting hounds after a rabbit. Someone got me for six dollars. It was a good thing I had most of my money in a leather belt around my waist.

A funny thing happened that day, in the mile race for

the sixteen-hand horses. They had a big horse named Sea-sick. He looked like the sea does on a windy day, a most peculiar whitish-gray pinto with thousands of little black dots all over him. He was a long shot, twenty-five to one. Several fellows, miners and hustlers, had him placed to win. The race started with thirty horses. They galloped the first half mile, with Seasick holding the out-side rail, fifth horse from the lead. On the three-quarter lap, the riders began closing in and pushing them out. Seasick kept creeping up, and at the last quarter home stretch he bolted and was coming up in the lead. The jockey riding him had been told that whatever he did he mustn't let Seasick win, so he pulled the horse to the in-side rail and jumped off him. The jockey landed in the field inside of the mile circle track. Seasick won the race by himself without a rider, by two lengths, but he was disqualified. The jockey must have known what he was doing, for he never could have stopped going the way that horse was headed. He crossed the field, then the track, and disappeared out of the Fair Grounds. After the fair, Helena grew very dead. The Capitol City lost all of its speed and pep for me. I decided it was not like a big city should be. Everyone seemed to know each other, like they did at home, so I returned to White Sulphur Springs.

CHAPTER 6

JOHN RINGLING COMES TO WHITE SULPHUR SPRINGS

JOHN RINGLING, the Circus man and Railroad builder, came out in his private Pullman car with five guests, Mr. and Mrs. L. N. Scott of St. Paul, Fred Loomas of Chicago and the Warden of Joliet, Illinois, and his wife, Mr. and Mrs. Allen. (She was killed later by Chicken Joe, a trusty convict in Joliet prison.)

John Ringling had built the branch line from Ringling, Montana, on the Chicago, Milwaukee and St. Paul, to White Sulphur Springs—twenty-three miles. His was the first private car I had ever seen and it gave me the travelling blues.

I was chauffeur for the Smith River Developing Company. Ringling was president. They had 90,000 acres of land, so it fell on me to drive the guests out on the mountain trails in a big seven-passenger air-cooled Franklin Six. They were amazed at the beauty of the valley and surprised to know that I didn't use a horn to warn people on the road. Warbling was one of my best stunts. I also held honors for calling soock, when salting cattle. Not having any occasion to make the soock call, I used this call for warning the travellers on the road, as no native could or would let an Easterner come in and get away without pulling his best stunt.

The Ringling party only stayed ten days. During that time there was one thing that happened that showed me very plainly that Easterners were people of power and conviction any time they had money. The Governor of Montana had a business engagement with John Ringling at eleven o'clock in the morning. Although awakened many times, Ringling was not up yet, and didn't get up until one-thirty. The Governor was six men, he was so hot. . . . But he waited. I made up my mind then that the West was fine, but I wanted to be an Easterner.

After they left, I bored Mother to death about the Big Cities and how I wanted to go to them. I told her how grand Ringling's guests told me it was to be in a big city. But no matter how bright I could paint my picture, Mother could always spot it out with a kettle of black. For consolation I would fall into some of the sporting houses of Joy along five in the evening—their breakfast time, at which time the girls and their sweetbacks would be holding convention, setting plans for the coming evening's battle, discussing how prospects for prosperity were always better in some other town. They talked of millionaires, steam-heated flats and white lights, all of which seemed to set my brain afire.

Many a time the conversations became so interesting that I almost died from anxiety had it not been that some bully sweetback would begin to threaten his girl that if she didn't turn in more money, he would import some red hot baby from Helena or Butte to take her place. Then the girl would cuss him for all she was worth, and maybe hit him over the head with a quart

beer bottle. This was more than apt to bring the following remark from the would-be bad man: "Aw, Honey,
can't you take a joke?"

There were some iron-bound women out there. I *mean*!

May Cooper, weighing only one hundred and five
pounds, could whip any pimp in town. No cop ever
locked her up. May Leamon, a big, half-breed Indian,
six feet tall with a shape like Venus, could spit higher
and holler louder than any woman on the line. She never
lost a battle of any kind. Whenever you saw her black
and blue, you knew someone else was in bed.

After a big row in the crib with his girl, you could
hear the sweetback, in one of the saloons, gloat over how
he treated his women. These men took great pleasure in
telling of the way they beat some woman up.

I was in Dan Smith's saloon, standing at the bar
drinking beer one day, when in came a stranger. The
place was almost empty save for old Ed McKay who
was sitting back against the south wall along side of a
big slot machine, propped up in an armchair, asleep,
with his mouth open. Willie Reed was tending bar. Henry Mason, a sweetback who boasted of gallant deeds,
and a fellow from Dorsey, were sitting at one of the
round card tables, playing crib. There was a big iron
stove about six foot high, with a rail running around it,
upon which the idlers rested their feet before a hot wood
fire. This stove stood in the center of the saloon. Dan's
saloon was thirty feet wide and sixty feet deep, with
mounted elk, antelope, and buffalo heads all along the

walls and one over the bar. He had a swell bar setting, too; billiard and pool tables—a nice place.

The stranger was dressed in a yellow corduroy suit—brand new. He looked around the place, then ordered a drink for the house. He hollered at Ed McKay who was asleep, but Willie Reed protested, saying, "For God's sake! Don't wake that pest up!" Henry Mason and his friend stepped to the bar. We all drank to the stranger's health. He talked of the city from whence he had just come—Harlowton. Henry Mason cut in with a knowing smile on his face. "Oh yes!" he said, and began telling of how much money he'd made in that place and how he had gotten into a fight with a drunken man there. He told how he had gouged out his eye, then laughed about it, rather boastingly.

The stranger's face turned red. He looked at Henry's reflection in the big mirror back of the bar. Without saying a word, he turned and slapped Henry right in the face—*Bowah!* At the same time, he pulled from a scabbard under his left arm a thirty-two special set on a forty-five frame, pointing it at Mason. "You're a fine bastard, to poke out a man's eye with your thumb. I ought to kill yah," he said.

Henry started to talk back, but the stranger said, "Shut up, or I'll blow your yellow heart out," and just to let Mason know he'd shoot, he turned the darned thing aloose and it cracked like a four-horse whip. The bullet hit right in the center of the slot-machine, that old McKay was propped up against, asleep. The broken glass from the effect of the bullet gave him a shower bath. He woke up, scared out of his wits, and ran out the side door, taking screen, hinges and all with him.

The stranger walked out.

Henry Mason was sick at the stomach with fright. The rest of us laughed as though to crack our sides, knowing that Mason would need a change of clothes. A timid mind has a peculiar action on the bowels.

*   *   *

At that time, I had lots of driving trips around the state, working for Ringling's land company, and on off days I drove other people's cars on long trips. These long trips became more profitable and interesting than my steady work with the land company, so I quit Ringling and drove private.

In those days, a chauffeur out there was no good on a long trip unless he could fix a car up if it broke down on the road. Town drivers never set out on the trails without someone who knew all about the engine with them.

I shall never forget the night I pulled over the Divide, going to Butte by way of Helena. We left Helena in the morning, but the people I was driving had to stop along the way to examine quartz at different mines. The sinking sun had just cast a dark shadow over the deep canyons, and the big headlights were making beautiful white streaks through the timber. The steady barking of my well-tuned unmuffled motor was music to my ears. While we were climbing the grade, I had noticed flashes lighting up the clear sky, like sheet lightning on a dark night,

but with a little more pinkish hue. I had heard people tell of the great sight it was to see from the train as it wound its way around the mountain at night, the flashing, snorting lava running smelters of Butte and Anaconda. But none of the imaginary pictures painted in my mind ever thrilled me as the real sight did that night. I stopped the motor, and put out the headlights, and stood viewing this sight from a high rock over a cliff beside the road for ten minutes. Probably I would have stayed longer if my guests had not gotten impatient.

I found Butte as a city was on the scale of most Montana cities, only it was the largest one I had been to so far. We returned home by way of Yellowstone National Park.

CHAPTER 7

NEVER SIT ON A GREEN SPOT NUDE

IN White Sulphur there had been for some time a movement led by Isaac Irkson, a Swede who couldn't speak
much English, and who was an undertaker. This movement was to drive all the sporting women out of town.

He had pulled an unusual campaign and succeeded in
having the Board of Aldermen to sign the papers. In a
month's time all the girls were out of town, and the
sporting houses closed. The town grew deader than a
door nail. The ranchers, miners and sheep herders went
every way but to White Sulphur. Only a few respectable
people complained, although their loss of business was
enormous. Naturally, some of the part-time compensated
companions to special women, who held themselves in
exalted positions, complained; in fact, they held nightly
beefs: they got drunk about it.

Irkson and his friend had two nieces to come to White
Sulphur, Olga and Elfrieda, not bad looking girls and
in their teens. Irkson kept them penned up in the house
continually, never allowing them hardly a breath of air.
Finally, an old lady who was somewhat of a community
worker and uplifter, thought the girls should have a
woman's care. Every once in a while she called on the
girls. They could not speak English, so that gave Irkson
a good opportunity to tell the old lady that her services

were not needed; that he could teach them all they needed to know.

The old lady's intuition told her that something was wrong, but she went away, not returning again for months. When she did return Irkson would not let her in, so she sought aid from the Sheriff. They gained admission. Her mind was right. Both girls were about to be confined. Both Irkson and his friend were jailed. When they were brought up for trial, who happened to be sitting on the bench but one of the same complaining young men, who used to get a good allowance from one of the former special women, one of the landladies on the line that Irkson had run out of town. The young man put in some good work on that jury, and the result was that they were found guilty of a grave misdemeanor; so the judge gave them the full extent of the law—Irkson, twenty years, and his friend, Julian, ten.

Never sit on a green spot nude unless you know your botany.

CHAPTER 8

TEMPERING MY NERVES

MOTHER was always hard pressed for money to keep her family going. We boys helped as much as we could. Bob and I were the hunters, for none of the other boys could hit the broad side of a barn with a double-barrelled shot gun. George was the best fisher. Jim Omar owned the Meat Market. His slaughter house was just outside the city limits on the north center side of town. Smith River ran twenty feet from it. Most of the poor kids used to go down to the slaughter house on killing evenings, and help Oscar Singer, the butcher, dress beef, lamb and pork. Their pay was brains, liver and tripe.

I'll never forget Oscar. He was six feet four in his stocking feet, wore a seventeen collar and number thirteen shoes. He brought six pairs of wooden shoes from Germany, and he wore them at slaughtering time. He could speak but little English. He could kill a steer with one blow of an ax and pick up a three-hundred pound pig with one hand; drank hot beef blood, fresh from the jugular vein of a bleeding steer, saying that blood put the thick hair on his chest. We got along fine with him. He was idolized by us all until *East Lynne* came to town, played by a road company in the Auditorium on the hill. Everybody attended, including Oscar Singer.

All the kids sat in the front part of the hall—the front three rows of benches; then came their parents. On the last two rows of benches sat the cowpunchers, miners and boys who thought themselves men, in which class I then was. They all sat on top of the benches with their feet on the seat.

Oscar Singer was sitting on the right hand side of the house, a few feet from the Red Hickory—the wood stove, which was so called because it was a Hickory make and always had a red side when there was a fire in it.

The curtain went up. The show began and all the kids were as quiet as mice, as they always were at the beginning of any show, good or bad.

East Lynne proved too heavy for us would-be men, so we began looking for amusement elsewhere. Julius Brug spied Jack Rees sitting beside his mother and crying because she was crying. Surely a boy eight years old couldn't understand *East Lynne*! Especially a Catholic Sunday School boy. That started us to snickering. A few hushes from older people in front of us put a damper on that.

Everything was going along fine until right in the most touching part of the play—the part where either the mother or mother-in-law (I forget which) is to take the young man for herself. Of course, as you know, that was terrible and a great sacrifice. But what she had in mind to do was good. The actress playing that part was very beautiful, tall and slender, sort of Gibson features. All in all, if it had not been for her gray wig and black dress, she would have looked too young to be a mother or mother-in-law. All over the place you could hear people crying. I couldn't understand why such a holler was put up about the idea. I had seen much better looking young men taken away by homelier women than she. The whole thing was too deep for us. I happened to turn my head to the right and what did I see but Oscar, the butcher, the ox-killer and blood-drinker, shaking with grief and tears arolling down his great big face! I jabbed Julius in the ribs with my elbow. Seeing what I saw, he looked at me, and I at him, amazed for a few seconds. Then we screamed out into wild laughter, breaking up the show.

That night, without any warning, mother, waiting until I was in bed, dragged me out for my last clubbing from her. I spent a sleepless night. My mind roamed to every place that I had studied in geography. I thought that any place must be better than home with such treatment, and people without any sense of humor. I even thought it better to be dead.

The following week L. N. Scott sent me a telegram, wiring me a ticket to St. Paul, Minnesota, to be his chauffeur. I packed my bag, although under heavy protest from my mother, also many other folks about town, who prophesied sickness, starvation, jail, even death. I must face all these. From personal experience, I knew something of each, except death, although I had seen that overtake many an animal and bird. Didn't I see something of contentment in the lines of their lifeless bodies as they laid before me? I had learned that there was beauty in death, if you looked for it. What difference did it make where it overtook me?

64

So, one glorious September morning, the eleventh, 1910, found me riding the eastbound Chicago, Milwaukee and St. Paul Railroad, my cheap suitcase packed with shirts, socks, underwear and overalls and an extra pair of pants that did not exactly match the suit I wore. In my pocket was forty dollars. In my mind was 286 Nelson Avenue, St. Paul.

While looking out of the window of the day coach, watching the blue peaks of the Rockies disappear behind me, my mind turned to the last instructions Mother and friends had given me. Many of them I neglected, but one thing Mother told me I heeded, that I didn't need my forty-five in the city, so I had left it behind. Why? The thought came to me as the train rambled farther and farther from home, and I began to feel alone. I always felt safe anywhere with Blue Steel Betty by my side: she gave me courage and protection at home when I was alone. They had pictured nothing but trouble in the city, still they convinced me that my forty-five would mean the worst. My nerves grew shaky.

Had I been on a saddle-horse at that moment, I might have turned back. But instead, I had to look at the fast moving ground and bid farewell. I mumbled to myself, Good-bye, sharp tops and deep canyons. I may never see you again, nor the heavy foliage that covers you, painted different hues by the rising and setting sun. No more shall I see the speckled trout hit at a fly-hook from behind a twig in rushing waters, or taste their delicious flesh, when it comes curling fried from a hot rock. I shall miss the bark of the pistol and the thud of a bullet when it brings down a blue grouse. I wondered if they rolled blue grouse in mud, feathers and all, then baked them in hot ashes in the city.

My melancholy musing might have lasted indefinitely had it not been for a noisy news-butcher selling his wares. He had a game to show me where I could get rich quick. It was only fate that I didn't pay him forty dollars for the idea. The train stopped at a town where a half-breed Indian got on: he sat down in a vacant seat across from me. When the train started again the news-butcher was coming through the car, with the intention to show me the fine points of the game. But it seems he had shown the same game to the half-breed sometime before for seventy-five dollars. It had proved unsuccessful, and the Indian wanted his money back. Because of that, I nearly witnessed my first murder! It was the conductor who straightened them out. The act proved to me that my old friend of the Hills—C. H.—was right: "Never play another man's game."

After another uneasy night, it was eleven o'clock in the morning when the train stopped in St. Paul. Mr. Scott's chief engineer of the Metropolitan ·Theatre was there to meet me. He took me to Mr. Scott's residence on Nelson Avenue, where Mrs. Scott greeted me. She showed me my room, then the engineer gave me instructions about the Locomobile I was to drive. Scott, who was in Minneapolis at the time, had a large private garage in his back yard.

After I found myself in the big city, I wasn't sure that I would like my job in it. Things seemed to be done so queer. A time was set for everything, and not the best hours, according to my judgment. Breakfast at 7:30, feeding the dogs at 8:00, take Mr. Scott to the office at 9:00, lunch at 1:00, to Minneapolis at 2:00 and 8:00 P. M. Everything timed. They even did it to time. Had it not been that Mr. and Mrs. Scott were such nice people, I would have left the first morning, because Pernhagen told me so many things I would have to do on time.

My first trip with the car was taking Mr. Scott to the office the following morning. To me, it seems as though St. Paul was laid out by a cross-eyed Frenchman, following a milk cow's tail, so you can judge how the streets run. After inquiring from a couple of cops, I managed to get back to 286 Nelson Avenue. That afternoon Mrs. Scott had me take her shopping, and to a few other places I should know the roads to. I was used to mountain trails, so I learned St. Paul and Minneapolis streets quickly.

One afternoon I took Mrs. L. N. to a beauty parlor— I should say hair-dresser, for at that time she was one of the most naturally beautiful women in St. Paul, for the newspapers had quoted her as being so. While waiting for her, I had a little pain in my stomach. I decided to step in a restaurant and get a bite to eat. I sat at the counter while the waiters ran up and down by me like white mice in a cage. It was in this restaurant I learned that the magic power of Uncle Sam's money didn't respond to me. Never before had I had plenty of the attractive paper and weights in my pockets, taken them out and laid them down for anything reasonable, that what I had desired to exchange them for didn't come a-hopping.

I saw the bill-o'-fare hanging up on the wall with many things listed. At the bottom was "Fresh Homemade Apple Pie and Milk—25 c." in large letters. I laid two bits down on the counter and as one of the waiters passed me, I said, "Give me apple pie and milk, please." He began getting red around his collar, then the redness quickly mounted to the top of his bald head, catching the ends of his ears. Then he grew deathly pale except for the lobes of his ears. Finally, he spoke. "We don't serve colored people in here." That was the first time I had ever heard that phrase, and I really didn't quite understand him, so I answered, "Just pie and milk."

Then he lost control of himself, picked up my money, throwing it at me with this remark: "Get to hell out of here. Don't you understand? Niggers can't eat in here."

Even at that I couldn't get it through my head why he should be mad at me. I hadn't done anything, but I knew he was hot. My right hand automatically fell to my left hip where old Betty always hung when I was alone. She wasn't there! I can't describe the lonely feeling that came over me. I have never felt like it since. It seemed as though everyone whom I knew had died at once.

Something told me that if I didn't move, I would have a fight. With boys at home, battles were head and head, but with a man, I felt I'd have little chance barehanded, so out I walked, cranked up the big Loco and drove to the Metropolitan Opera House to see Tom Owens, the footman and porter. He had told me before that there were a lot of things that he must tell me in order that I might get along in the East. Tom had been a prize fighter and had travelled lots. I found him polishing the long brass railing which led to the balcony.

At sight of me he said, "What's up? You seem to be all upset." In some way he could tell that I wasn't myself. I told him what had happened. He laughed, "Hee Hee"—an act that was done through his nose in high tones—then said, "Man, don't you know you's a niggah and can't do things heah like you did out home in Montana?"

I asked him to tell me all the inside stuff on this thing, nigger and niggah. I found myself to be pronouncing it again and again. I was sure the waiter had called me and all like me niggers and Tom had said niggah. Then I showed him the quarter I had laid on the counter. His answer to it all was that white people who wanted to be nasty called anyone like me with curly hair, thick lips and black skin, "niggers," but most any colored person would call you "Niggah," a word taken from an exalted ruler of Abyssinia, and not have any evil thought in mind at the time he said it. As for the lady on the quarter I showed him, he said that in a white man's hands she was a goddess, but in my hand she was a bogus bitch.

My time was up so I returned for the Madam. Tom's last words were for me to come to the flat any night, and that he'd tell me anything I would need to know to get along in the East; not to pay any attention to that waiter. I thanked him, as I was glad to learn.

The Madam was waiting for me in front of the hair-parlor, and as the car stopped she inquired whether or not I had been to another fire. I told her yes, but this time the fire was in my mind, at the same time nodding toward the restaurant. She asked my complaint. When I related to her the incident, a beautiful red tint came over her prized face as she answered, "Oh yes, I should have told you before of the different opinions of people in the U. S. A. If you drive slowly up Summerset Avenue, I'll tell you the things most essential for you to know." In two hours' time I got an emancipated Eastern woman's ideas and advice, in order that I might be enlightened. Many things that Mother might have told me but didn't, and that Sis read but couldn't understand, were told to me.

Our conversation made me more anxious to find out everything that Tom knew, so that night twelve o'clock caught me at Tom's flat. Two girls were there—one fair with light brown hair and blue eyes, and the other a fat walnut-brown. Tom introduced me as a kid from the West, a real greenhorn. They poked much fun at me. Tom had told them of my day. Many questions I asked, then I told them of my ambition to become a great electrician and inventor, which brought forth loud laughter, only to be smothered up by guzzling drinks. Both girls were greatly amused, the fairest one seeming to get the most fun at my expense.

She told me of her travels and ambitions: how they

had all turned out to be mush because she couldn't let spades alone; that she would work as a white girl until a brown came to town and she got mixed up with him, which would cause her boss to accuse her of being a white girl nigger-lover, and ball her out. Then she would tell the boss she was colored, which would make it worse.

She told me that the best thing I could do was to go to New Orleans, where a lady conducted a school teaching young bucks like me how to be a real sweetback, and that was the best job any white man would let me have, (loving), and that it had to be on the sly. What she said was hard for me to believe, and her ideas were absurd as far as I could see. Hadn't I spent years in Montana around that kind of business, seeing all nationalities of men as lovers of women, and didn't I know that no real wealth had been acquired in that way? I told her that I knew all about that, but she answered by saying that I knew everything but the East and Niggahs. Then she became silent for a while. When she did speak again, she said, "Oh, well; go ahead. You'll find out what good jobs you'll get."

The door bell rang; some Pullman porters and a sweetback had come to call on Tom. Old friends met, and there was lots of gay greetings. One of the porters spoke up suddenly, "Hello, Tom!" Tom looked surprised and hollered, "God damn your old soul! Well, if it ain't old Mack!" and, turning to one of the other men, said, "Bennie, where da hell didja get this niggah from? I ain't seen him for five years."

Bennie was the King of the Sweetbacks in St. Paul,

having women that gave him as high as a thousand dollars at a time, when their fingers were busy and lucky. He was known as the roughest, best-looking spade in St. Paul, and a gambler from his heart. He changed clothes three times a day. He answered Tom in a clear, baritone voice. "Oh, these spades fell in to Fan's Club and broke up the crap game; you know I wouldn't let these niggahs leave St. Paul with all the money they've won, so I'm taking them around to meet some of the gals. They might turn some of it aloose to them, and I'll pick it up by and by. Ha! Ha!" His laugh at the close of his speech started off the second joyous outbreak for the evening. More drinks were passed and the group became congenial.

Tom inquired what kind of gals they wanted. One of the porters who had been silent up to this time even at the introduction, spoke up. "Kinds? Yah don't tell me yah have *kinds* of women around heah, does yah?" "Well, not exactly *all* kinds, but all colors and most all reasonable. Ain't that right, Tom?" said Bennie. Then with his characteristic laughter, he started the noise off again, continuing his talking. "If pretty white, black, or brown women can't get it from you, I'll go to Minneapolis and get you a Chinese woman. But that will cost plenty of money, I think—more than you want to spend."

The brown skin gal broke in, saying, "Yes, scarcity makes things high, and thank God there ain't many browns in St. Paul like me. Hee! Hee!" And with that she rocked back in the rocking chair, showing her plump legs and starting out a fresh burst of laughter.

"Yes, boys; that's rare color up heah," Tom hollered from the kitchen.

"*Too* rare. You can't get to her for the peckerwoods. I's always wanted her on my string but she can't see me," Bennie commented.

"I sees you, Bennie, and I sees your string. I sees you beat one of your gals one night down to Fan's, too. If a man would beat me like you beat her, I'd kill him and die for it," the big brown said.

Bennie smiled with ego, and stated as follows: "There ain't no woman that I got who wants to see me dead, nor die herself unless I kills her with love. You seed what she did, didn't yah? Gimme all her money and *begged* me to take her home. And I done it. And when *I takes 'em home, they're happy* . . . and you'd be the same."

At the end of his speech, he slapped the brown on her plump hip. She reached for a cigarette in silence. . . . A burning cigarette is cooling to a hot bottom.

"Damn all this argument about what you all wants. You knows what *we* wants, so get busy an' produce the goods," came from one of the porters.

"Take your time, man; it's early yet," Tom said, as he came into the room with a tray full of fresh drinks.

"Yes, but they're right, Tom. That's why I brought 'em by heah. All my best gals are busy. I knowed you could always get your stuff on the wire," Bennie remarked, and then, turning to the gang, he continued comfortingly, "Tom ain't got nothing but part-time gals. They works all over town—just good-time gals. Ain't going to cost you a fortune, you know."

Tom stepped to the telephone to get a number. While the operator was getting his number, he turned to the three porters and said, "I only need two more gals. This gal's a regular fellow," pointing to the fair girl. "Turn that white light out and look at her in a soft light. . . . That's it. See, you can't tell her from a beautiful ofay."

"Maybe not in a soft light, but when I'm feeling my drink, Uuumm—M—HM! you can tell in the dark," the fair girl answered, stretching her arms above her head.

Tom finally got his number and in speaking to the party at the other end, said, "Hello! Is that you Dolly? Can you an' Mag come over? A couple of my old friends are in town."

Several things must have been said on the other end of the line, because Tom continued, impatiently, "Oh, yes—you know I wouldn't send you into any other kind. . . . Ring the bell two short rings. Yes, yes—sure, all-right. Good-bye," and hung up.

He broke the silence in the room by saying, "Now don't you guys fall in love with my gals, and try to ship 'em out of town with yahs."

"Don't worry 'bout that. We picks our birds where we kills 'em, and we leaves our bones where we eats 'em," one of the porters moaned.

Bennie turned to me and spoke to me for the first time. "Say, Kid; why are you so quiet? Damn! you been sitten heah like a church mouse ever since we rolled in. You ain't deaf and dumb are yah?" Before I could answer, he swung around to Tom and exclaimed, "Tom! You didn't get a gal for the kid!"

"Oh, hell, no! White gals wouldn't excite him. He's what you call a black-peckerwood, raised up here in Montana. I don't know his reputation with women, besides, he's pritty young. I ain't maken any mistakes—disappointing any my gals by sending in a greenhorn on 'em," Tom said.

"For Christ's sakes! You don't mean to tell me here's a young niggah that don't know how to love a woman, do yah?" Bennie asked.

"All young boys must learn to treat a lady nice," the fair girl said.

"Damned if *I* needed any lessons. I was treating 'em nice before I left Country School, fourteen years old," Bennie boasted.

"Yes, but that was down south, where it's hot. Kids get started earlier there. He's from away up north where the land is covered with Ice and Snow," Tom explained.

"Hell! that cuts no ice. He's a niggah, ain't he? There ain't no weather that's supposed to stop a niggah from maken love. The white man says so, an' I proves his statement. You know it gets cold as hell heah," Bennie protested, bursting into laughter, then, stopping it by filling his mouth with whiskey and water. When he got his breath he said to me, "Kid, I want to talk to you. You're a big buck. I can use you if you follow my instructions."

Just then the door-bell rang. Tom answered it. Two girls come in. They reminded me of Jewell Hooks, with a little more pretenacious air of women. Right away I knew what Tom and Bennie meant by "good-time gals."

More drinks were passed. Informal introductions. Laughter. Bennie started telling one of his risky stories. Soon everyone was congenial. A game started—a game called "Shake, rattle an' roll for five," as I bid good-night.

On the way home, my mind began to analyze city ways. Much about niggahs and peckerwoods was spilled in my brain. I needed the walk up Summet Hill. Once before in my life, I had had the experience of being drunk. That was when a gang of us went fishing through the ice on a Sunday. We had a dozen bottles of Duffy's Malt they sold at that time in the drug stores. We made an agreement that every time we caught a fish, we'd take a drink! We tramped all day before we caught one out of a beaver dam, on our way back to the team. C. H. Sherman was the first one to cut a hole in the ice. When he dropped his line in, a trout tried to jump out of the ice. He hollered with joy, for we hadn't taken a drink all day. Ina hour's time, we caught over a hundred fish, and all the Duffy's Malt was gone. We hitched up and started for home. Before we had driven five miles, I was owl-eyed. That same feeling was coming over me now. I made it to Scott's house ina few minutes an' stole quietly upstairs to my room.

In bed, I began to take myself serious. All the grand things I had planned to be were pipe-dreams. They couldn't be done! Then all my nicknames came to me—Snowball, Zip and Blacky. But they called Jimmy Keen "Blacky" too, and really the only thing black about him was his hair. Besides, with all my nicknames, none of them made any difference about where I ate or slept. It baffled me to think that the mask that aided me so much at home, was all against me in the cities I dreamed of. Sleep over-took me.

The next morning I felt kinda blue. But one must be a good shot, if they want to skin a Gopher, or mount a Baldheaded Eagle. Never did I see either one of them lay down when they were hurt, so why should I? My wounds were not bleeding to remind me I had them. So I soon forgot my first battle in the big city.

Mrs. Scott was upset to think I had spent most of the evening in not the best of company. She suggested for me to make the acquaintance of some nice colored girls that went to church in St. Paul.

When I asked Tom about this, he was much opposed to the idea, unless I wanted to get married.

Marriage was a thing I had thought of a few times when girls at home had given me the headache (what old folks call child love) but because of all the tales I had heard and sights I had seen, for me marriage would be an absolute failure without money. In my imagination, lots of money and great success at something I like to do is the two-humped camel that I would like to ride. I thought to myself Mrs. Scott's idea would lead to marriage. Awh no. Church girls were out for me.

But every niggah in St. Paul had a sweetie of some kind; sweetbacks had chains of them, all nationalities. If I wanted to call myself a man, living right, I had to get a gal, the gang said.

The luck I had! Can you fancy me finding a long, tall,

olive-brown, with eyes that had a moisted expression—
gave one the idea she was kind-hearted? But a woman
harder to get on with never lived. Not once in the ten
months that I supported her did she consent to go any
place I suggested. If I said "Let's go to a show"—"Oh
no! Dance tonight," she'd say.

"Chop Suey?"

"Nope, Chicken."

"Auto ride?"

"My Gawd, no. Cabaret tonight."

She always had her way, until one night they were
having a dance in St. Paul, at the Mecca Hall. I told
her about it a month ahead of time. She said she would
go at the time I spoke to her about it. On the night of the
dance, she came with a long cock and bull story 'bout how
the St. Paul affair would be the Jinks. Whereas they were
giving one in Minneapolis that would be the Berries.

She went to the Minneapolis party. I went to the St.
Paul ball.

There was a wicked brown at that ball, who taught
me to never let no one companion worry my mind. The
charming olive-brown and I split up for good that night,
and I considered myself a lucky fellow, much wiser.

A few weeks later, when a bunch of us chauffeurs
were waiting at the theatre, they told me I was the only
colored driver in town, and all the wealthy people on
Summit Avenue would like to have me, any time I quit
the Scott job. The man-killer job, they called it, because
L. N. kept such late hours. I had lots of faith in their
talk, especially after what had happened to me one day

when I was coming from Minneapolis, by the river route. It was this way.

A young lady dressed to kill had stalled her nice Pierce Arrow roadster in six inches of mud. She hailed me to get her out of the mess. I gallantly waded out and started the motor. She thanked me and gave me her address and 'phone number, and then, after a pause, said, "Father gave me this car last week. Won't you teach me all about it?"

I accepted the job. She agreed to take her first lesson at any time I might have off. A couple days later, in the afternoon, we were on a lonely road. She was having her first lesson. I found her a very apt pupil. She never drove zig-zagging like most new drivers do. We stopped under a shady tree for a rest, and I told her tales of the west. . . . Before the course was over, we learned to be good pals.

A Grand Opera Company was playing in St. Paul. She said her mother and father were going to it, but she would stay home if I would come over. I agreed. At 9:10 that evening, I was walking into their wealthy mansion. We each had a well mixed cream d' mint high-ball, while we conversed, sitting ona large divan in the lounging room. Although the divan was very soft, the atmosphere of the room was very heavy. She seemed to feel it too, because her conversation scattered into silence. She looked around the room, and then suddenly jumped as if an idea had hit her, and, with a broad smile, said, "I have some pictures I want to show you. They are in a large album in my room. I think it will be much nicer to

79

go up there and see them. It's too big to move down here."

We got up and left the room, ascending the stairs to-gether slowly, and, at the top of the stairs, turned to the left into her palacial boudoir. She closed the door behind us gently. The soft lights made me know Maude Heal-dyne must of had some contact with blooded people, and maybe her tales about her great English parents were true.

We sat in a large plush chair big enough for two. She asked me more about the west. As we talked low, the tales of the out-door life thrilled her. Suddenly, she real-ized she hadn't showed me the pictures. As she raised to get the Album, a tapping was heard on the heavy door, followed by a cultured voice calling, and trying the knob in close successions of seconds.

"Margret, Mar-*gretta*—It's mother, darling," the voice called. Margret was scared speechless and didn't answer. I looked at the door. I couldn't see how it was locked. I looked for an exit. There was none but the window. Something told me, by the way her mother re-peated her rapping on the door, I should not get caught in Margret's bedroom.

I quietly raised the window and hung out. Margret pulled it down almost shut. Then she answered her mother's call, as if just wakened from sleep.

"Yes! yes! Yes, oh—oh, *yes;* mother," she said.

"Open the door!" came the reply from the mother.

Margret opened the door, as I hung there by my hands, afraid to breathe.

Through the almost shut window, I heard her

mother explain that she had taken a beastly headache in the Opera and came home. The maid was out and she wanted Margret to unhook her tight-fitting black lace dress.

It was pitch dark outside, and I couldn't see how far my feet were from the ground, or what was under me. Suddenly, an automobile came around the corner, with big head-lights. They lit up the whole house. I could see the ground. My feet were fully three yards from it. I couldn't hang there like a scarecrow, so I let go and hit the ground arunning, clearing the six-foot back fence in one vault. Then I disappeared in the darkness.

I have often wondered what was in that Album.

* * *

Good farmers plant their seeds early.

CHAPTER 9

EARLY TRAINING BEARS ITS FRUITS

IN St. Paul, much had been said to me about the Twin Cities being small burgs. Chicago, St. Louis, and Kansas City were the cities for spades (another name meant for me and all my kind) according to those who had lived in those places. None of them mentioned New York City.

I asked Mrs. L. N. Scott of that town, and she said, "Oh! You mustn't call New York City a town. That's the largest city in all the United States." Then she cold-watered it to me by adding, "Nowhere else one needs so much money to live with, as they do in New York."

"Money! Is *that* all?" I asked.

Before I could get another word from her, the 'phone rang. Mr. Scott was calling for me to come to the office and bring him home. While on the way, I thought to myself, if all Eastern cities are like St. Paul, money need not bother me, because I can't spend it as I want to, even if I have plenty of it. Railroad fare was all I needed. I made up my mind to quit and get some of the better jobs the white chauffeurs told me about. I could make extra money with more spare time, and see the big cities quicker.

I quit the Scott job, and tried to find one of them, to get the names and addresses of some of the people who were so anxious to give me a job. None of that gang of chauffeurs were to be found any place, the funniest thing you ever experienced. They had all disappeared like flies in the wintertime. I put an ad in the papers. No one answered but a Jap who ran a little chop-house, and the wages he offered me was a crime. I took my troubles to Tom. He told me I was crazy to quit a good job like I had, where I had nothing to worry about, and that there were only three things left for me to do: go home, be a railroad porter, or a Sweetback and Gambler. I accepted the truth of his statement, and in two weeks' time I was a Porter on a tourist car from Chicago to Portland, Oregon. I found myself at home on that job—there were so many women that rode from town to town, between St. Paul and the coast, who brought the stronger sex from the day coaches back into my car. I earned a nice fee from them, but there wasn't any real thrilling experiences on that type of car.

I made three trips before they put me on a chair car run from St. Paul to Duluth. That turned out *too* good for me: I made ten dollars on the trip, which excited me so that I told an old Ace, and he took my head. After that, I rode a Pullman from Chicago to the coast. On that run I was schooled in story telling by some of America's great unprofessional monologests—the travelling drummers. After a few trips on that class of car, they put me on a special train for the Pierceson Land Company, of Canada. They were sending people from all over the East to buy land in the Saskatchwan valley. Our train was made up of tourist, Pullman, private and dining-cars. The Land officials rode in the private cars.

I had seen lots of wheat fields, but none like I saw along the Red River valley: for miles and miles, the golden flags waved at us as we passed. At Saskatune, Canada, they backed our train out on a siding, almost out of town. There wasn't a house within eight blocks of it.

The next morning at six o'clock, men came with teams and wagons to take all these land-buyers out to the ground that was to be sold. In my car, there was a bride and groom from southern Ohio. Most all this mob of people loaded into these wagons and started off acrossed the hills like the parade in *The Covered Wagon*. Those that were not going (some ten or twelve) disappeared in all directions. When the last wagon ducked its hind wheels over the knoll, I returned to make up my car. Behold! in the hussel and bussel, I didn't notice that the bride hadn't gone. Her youthfull voluptious form lay propped up in the berth, on one elbow. One of her hands was holding the Pullman car window curtain at a slanting angle. She was watching the settling dust made by the wagon train that was carrying her husband of three days into the wilderness.

"Why! I thought you had gone with the lot," I said. She never answered me. Her eyes were focused out on the wilderness with a strange gaze. I had started to make up my car when she spoke.

"My Lord! I married him and he intends to settle down out here," she said.

I wouldn't comment on his actions, so I proceeded to clean up the car. There were a few minutes' silence. Then we had a little talk about where we were. Then

84

came silence again. She looked out the window once more, as if studying very hard. All the dust had settled. The grey hills rolled before her view. She layed back down again.

"A? A?—you—you know: you're the first Nig-nigger I have ever talked—talked to. Can I? I?—believe all— believe all my mother and father have told me about you people?" she inquired hesitatingly, with a peculiar smile.

Her remarks flashed through my mind, bringing with them things the boys had told me that white people say about niggahs, and I realized what she was suggesting. It's sure hard to make white people beleive that what they say might be true about some of us, but not about the whole race. Still, as the legend is to our advantage, I left my work for an hour, so that it shouldn't die with me.

* * *

That night the wagons and their human cargo returned to the cars about eight-thirty. Most of the people dined in the city of Saskatune. Nearly everyone that went up to buy land, bought, and some remained in Canada on that trip, including the married couple. The rest returned to Chicago. That was one of the poorest railroad trips I have ever made as a porter with passengers. The older porters on the trip knew how to get money out of that kind of a mob, but I didn't earn ten dollars on the week's trip, and I worked my head off.

The following week I was on a compartment-car, rolling toward the Pacific Coast again. I felt myself a full-fledged porter. I had an Ace's run, even if I did get it on account of his sickness. The trip out was interesting because I had a new phase of the Porter business—mixing drinks and selling sandwiches. Then, too, the berths were all in little rooms by themselves. The class of people were much different. They either had Money, or were after it in big lots at a time.

In Seattle, the porters would rush to buffet-flats or gambling-houses, and sometimes, to a movie show. I asked one why the colored people did not go to more places of interest, museums and legitimate shows. "White people only like a niggah when he's in his place, and they think a niggah's place is in the whore-house, gambling-den, or the cotton field," he informed me. "I'm a Niggah that knows his place. Come on, I know where there's some cute little Chinese gals," he added, as we left the car together.

It was my first trip to Seattle, and I thought I must see some of the streets of interest. When we left the railroad yards, my friend, who was leading, didn't turn toward the high buildings, so we split up. I walked from the railroad station to the heart of Seattle's business district, and during the short walk, there were three rainstorms and three sun-peeps over the shaggy hills. I was interested to learn, while talking to a stranger, that Chinese and Japanese ran big businesses; he also told me that Japanese ran many of the large businesses on the main streets. I attended the B. F. Keith vaudeville show that night. After the show, I went up to the section where the colored people live. I found the biggest business they had was a crap game over a Chinese restaurant, all nationalities playing. I had begun to think that was the main business sponsored by the people I was classed with. If I had not have known what a bad business deal it was, I might have set out to get myself a craphouse.

On the trip coming back, at Spokane, Washington, a fascinating lady boarded my car. Her manner was like that of a princess! Her navy blue hat matched her blue suit. The white lace hanging down around the brim interfered with a clear view of her eyes. The ticket she held called for state-room "C". She was the only state-room passenger I had going farther east. In a few minutes, the train jerked off in its usual way. The great jack was puffing out its mournfull sighs under its heavy load as we rolled on toward the rising sun.

It was five-thirty in the evening when the lady in room "C" first rang the bell for the porter. She asked for dinner to be served in her state-room. I always had a menu in my car; it saved me many a step. She wrote her order on a telegram blank, and when she handed it to me, I got my first look at her hatless head. The features were familiar, but I couldn't call her name to save me.

"Why are you looking at me so?" she asked.

"Pardon me, Madam, but I thought you were from White Sulphur Springs, Montana," I said.

"Well, I'm not from there, but I have been there. Surely *you* are not from there? There's only one colored famley in the town," she continued.

"I'm part of that famley. Mannie Gordon is my name," I answered.

With great surprise, she cried out, "My! But you have grown. Why, you were just that high" (holding her hand about four feet from the floor) "when I was last there."

"Yes? What were you doing there, or who were you with?" I asked.

"Oh, don't you remember me? I was with Maude Healdyne—Jewell Hooks, I was Jewell Hooks. But I'm Harriet Radclyffe now. Go and put in my order an' come back and talk to me," she said.

I followed instructions.

We talked of the old times when I was page, and of the old times in White Sulphur. She told me Maude was married to a rich man in San Francisco, and she herself was travelling for some large dress firm in Frisco; that she was on her way to Chicago, and that she didn't bother with men any more, unless they were the Real Thing.

"You know, of course—if that comes along," (rubbing her thumb on her first finger) "let me know," she said.

I nodded yes, just as the waiter rang the bell at the door, and came in with the food—tomato soup, lamb chops, mashed potatoes, peas, and head lettuce—no sweets, black coffee.

The train moved on. It looked like a bum trip for me, with only six men and two women, and they didn't ride far. The train was soon empty, except for Harriet Radclyffe, until eleven o'clock that night, as the train pulled out of Glacier National Park, where a new passenger got in my car.

He was a red-faced man, nearly six feet tall, richly dressed in tan nickers, coat and pants to match, a sport sweater and golf shoes on. Maybe he had seen forty-five summers, but not more.

"George, give me a Scotch high-ball," he ordered.

("George," I said to myself, "that's what the porters say a real Mr. Eddie an' Miss Ann calls a porter—'George!'")

I served the drink. He drank it like a man who hadn't had a drink of anything for a week.

"Ah! That's fine. Give me another one," he said, smacking his lips.

As I started for the drink, he pealed a twenty-dollar bill off his big roll. The way he carried his money, I knew he was the real thing. The second high-ball he took much more time to drink. I handed him the daily paper.

"That's it; you know what a man wants," he flattered me.

I walked out of the observation end of the car. I went into room "D", and from there, used my key to get into Harriet's room next door. She was in bed, asleep. I awaked her gently, and told her the Real Thing was on board, and what should I do? She was awake in a minute. "Don't say a thing. Just try to keep him up a little while longer," she said.

I left as I entered, to follow orders. When I got back to the buffet end of the car, my nice passenger ordered another drink. I took more time to get it ready than I did the first two. After serving the drink, I turned the lights down on the opposite end of the car, so he could read without the light shining in his eyes.

"That's fine," he grunted. "Kinda light this trip, aren't you?" he asked.

"Yes. Just you ana lady passenger in my state-rooms, since I left Spokane, and my last chair passenger got off when you got on," I answered.

"Lady? Ah! . . . Old?" he questioned, seeming interested.

"Late twenties, I judge," I answered.

"HUMMM!" he grunted, and laid his paper down.

Before either of us could speak again, Harriet, dressed in a loose-fitting old-rose Chinese silk robe, slipped through the door into the observation part of the car. She took a seat near the big back window. She absolutely ignored us. Not a word was spoken. I went to my pantry bunk and sat down.

In less than ten minutes, "Hummm—quiet trip, isn't it?" came from the gentleman, and "Yes it is—and I have a splitting head-ache, too," came from Harriet.

"Head-ache? Why, a little Scotch, lemon an' soda always cures my head-aches."

From my seat in the pantry, I heard him walking toward me, saying, "George! George! Get a little Scotch, lemon an' soda there, quick."

I jumped into service, handed him the drink and he served it to Harriet. I sat back down again.

They sat and talked as the coaches rocked on to the East. I couldn't understand all they said under their muffled tones, but I soon knew Harriet was feeling much better. I could tell by her laughter. They ordered more drink. I could see that Harriet was sitting in a way to make any man with red blood want to hold her in his arms. Once more I disappeared to my hidden seat, and wished they'd buy a dozen little bottles of whiskey and leave me go to sleep.

I heard Harriet scream gaily. Then she ran out of the observation into her state-room. The gentleman was right after her, but he was too slow. She had locked her door. He came back to me.

"George! George! Unlock that door," he said.

"What door?" I asked, as if I didn't know. "Your door is unlocked."

"Not mine, damn it; *her's!*" he shouted.

"Oh! I can't unlock the lady's door. Porters say a white woman will scream if they see a black face in the dark," I stalled.

"Scream? Hell! I'll protect you," he said, swaggering, and slapped a twenty-dollar bill into my hand.

I was convinced. "Well, you wait until I get out of sight, because if she sees me, she'll scream," I cautioned.

"Go ahead; be quick!" he said, knocking me through the door into the hall.

I went into the room "D" and used my key again. He was right on my heels. It was a good thing I knew Harriet, for he almost knocked me into her room before I could get out of his way.

* * *

Between Arroria and Chicago, Harriet rang the bell for the porter. She was making ready to get off in the windy city. We had a little chat about the gentleman that got off in Arroria. She thought I might need some new clothes, and asked if a hundred would fix me up. Smiles an' bows answered. As I handed her bag to the red-cap in the Union Station, her princess' figure tripped gracefully down the steps. We smiled at each other.

"I'm glad to have seen you again. I'm sure you'll be successful," I said.

"Thanks. Bye-bye. I shall tell Maude you are travelling, too," she said, turning away. I watched her disappear in the zig-zagging crowd of passengers, as they walked down the platform, out of the station.

The next trip an old porter took my head again, and I quit the railroad in St. Paul.

CHAPTER 10

GRATUITOUS SURPRISES

IN St. Paul, I got my experience as doorman and porter at the Orpheum Theatre. The work was not hard but continuous, every day and night. By being a chauffeur I earned good tips, handling people's cars. I was satisfied with life for some time. Things went unusually smooth for me.

Somehow or nother a church-going girl came into my life. Mother had pulled us kids to church so much when we were little, I hadn't attended any church since I had left home. I thought it would be a nice thing to take this girl to the Thanksgiven dinner they were going to serve in the basement of the Methodist church, at sixty cents a plate. That Thanksgiven morning caught me broke— not a soo in my pocket.

I remembered that, during the time I was railroading, I had loaned Guest, a tailor, thirty dollars to pay his house rent with. Two dollars of it I had gotten back. That was a coupla weeks after he had borrowed it. Guest owen me came to my mind. I thought if I could get a few more bucks out of him, I'd be all set for the day. I cleaned up my work in a hurry, and walked down to the station where Guest had his tailor shop. He was pressing a pair of pants. I sang him my hard luck tale.

"I only got two dollars myself, an' I need that to take my gal to the same thing," he said.

We talked a little while longer, and I started to leave, hoping to get the money some place else, when a porter came running to the door. He hollered out, "Heah, Guest! Take this two dollars an' gimme my coat. I gota chance to make extra." He threw the two-dollar bill down on the table, grabbed his coat and ran out of the shop. I felt good.

"Well, Guest, we're in luck. You got two bucks an' I got two," I said.

"I can't give you this two dollars; I need six to make the day with my gal," he declared, and grabbed up the money. We got into an argument. He told me lie after lie, saying he had to rent a room—when he hada house; must take a cab—when the street car ran right by the church door. It got hotter and hotter. He tried to hit me with a big clothes-pressing brush, fourteen inches long an' four inches wide. Somehow I got the brush an' cracked him over the head with it. He hollered murder. A big cop came into the shop. Guest knew more about pleading to a city cop than I did, so I got locked up.

I had to stay in jail all day Thanksgiven: the next day was Sunday—no court until Monday. Then the judge told me I couldn't take a debt out of a man's hide in St. Paul, and he gave me the choice of fifteen days or fifteen dollars.

I couldn't get in touch with any of my friends, so, with ten other prisoners, they loaded me in the Black Maria, hawled by two black horses, and carted us up to the work-house between St. Paul and Minneapolis. We were measured and weighed in. My cell mate was a Mexican, up for stabbing a man.

Before we were in the cell ten minutes, two men came along with old pie-tins (like mother used to feed baby chickens out of) loaded down with hunks of beef, boiled potatoes with their skins on, stewed tomatoes and half-stewed prunes, all on the same tin. We each got one. Following them was a fellow with a big bucket full of tin cups. Then came a man with a large garden sprinkler (no spray) full of sunburnt-black-asphelt coffee. He poked the pipe through the bars and filled our cups. I ate some of the garbage, but I couldn't go the coffee.

They were just getting ready to take me out on the rock pile, when Johnny Davis came and bailed me out.

The girl's parents stopped her from speaking to me.

* * *

Never try to compensate for gratuitous surprises.

* * *

I quit the theatre for a while, and got a busman's job at Uptown Charlie's restaurant, on Fifth Street, just across from the St. Paul Hotel. At that time, they had all colored waiters. Jim Hunt, a big six-foot yellow fellow, was the assistant headwaiter, and a young German was the headwaiter. I stayed there about a month. That was a job that meant long hours for a stomach full of food. They only paid ten dollars a week to the bus-boys. I never did get a chance to wait there—even on the help, so I quit and went to the roof of the St. Paul Hotel, as busman and waiter. I graduated there into getting a chance to feed the help, clerks and headwaiters. I couldn't keep room-rent off me at that job, so I quit again. The doorman at the Orpheum Theatre got sick, and I found myself back at the old job again, as footman. I was much better off at that. I couldn't break anything, and if I did, I didn't have to pay for it, like I did in the restaurants. I held this job for about a month and a half, during which time I got the feeling that St. Paul was too small. I must move on.

CHAPTER 11

NEW YORK BOUND

I SENT a telegram to John Ringling in New York City, asking him for a job of any kind. One evening about two weeks later, a telegram came from Ringling telling me to go to his Chicago office, get a pass and come to New York City. Naturally the message found me broke, so I went to L. N. Scott and showed him my telegram. He gave me fifty dollars for my fare, and regards to his friend J. R.

The following noon found me on the Burlington route, New York bound. From St. Paul to Chicago my trip was like a short trolley ride, so many thoughts ran through my head. Every one at home came before me in a vision. What would they say??? Emanuel Taylor Gordon—Mannie—Snowball—Old Zip—Blacky—in New York City—the biggest city in the U. S. A.! A feeling that comes once in a lifetime.

Getting off the train in Chicago put an end to my dreaming. I took a cab on my first trip over to the beautiful North side of Chicago. The clerks in the Ringling office at 221 Institute Place were very nice to me. They arranged that I was to leave on the Pennsylvania the following day as Mr. William Moran—the pass read that way.

I never felt bigger in my life, to be called Mr. Somebody, even if it wasn't my name. I had never been called Mr. Anything before. With a pass in my pocket, a bag in my right hand, raincoat over my left arm, I swaggered out of the office into a cab. "Drive me to the Pullman Hotel on South State Street," spoke Mr. Moran. The richest man in the world could not have layed back in a cab, more confident of his position in life, than I did that day. At the hotel I started to write MANNIE GOR-DON on the register. I got as far as M-A, when an infe-rior feeling came over me and I stopped, changed the A to R, followed by a period and W. Moran. No one knew me much in Chicago—why couldn't I be William Moran? The clerk said, "Room 12, Mr. Moran." I did not answer, just followed the bellhop with the key.

That night I went to a lowdown Negro show, at the old Pekin Theatre on South State Street. I wasn't up enough on Ethiopian phrases and most of the show went over my head. But there was something in their earthy dances and jokes that told me I must learn all about niggahs, because I was one of them, and to be one and not know something about them would be bad.

As I came out of the theatre, I met a fellow whom I knew while I was railroading to Chicago. When he learned I was on my way to New York City, he said, "Man, you may never see Chicago again. We'd better go out tonight". I told him I had my ticket and all my money on me, but if he would go with me to the hotel, where I could leave my pass and some of my money in the safe, I'd go with him, because between the theatre and the hotel, as I was walking near the buildings, two women gave me the bum's rush right into their bedroom. I cried "BROKE!"—not even fifty cents could I spend— so they let me out. He went to the hotel with me where I left my junk, and we stepped out.

I thought the whole south side of Chicago was one big Tenderloin. All kinds of women; nearly every house was mixed—all nationalities. It was difficult to explain to my friend that I wanted to learn about Colored People (as he called them). He was a graduate from one of the eastern universities. The railroad porter who introduced me to him told me he was a dickty spade, and that all dickty spades loathed the word NIGGAH, and for me never to use it in his presence.

We dropped into a couple of earthy cafes, but they were not exciting: just mixed drinking crowds—men and women, telling stories. Then we went to a few houses where they had eight or ten mixed girls. They were too near like what I was used to on Main Street at home. I wasn't happy, so asked my friend to take me where they made up the songs, and real black velvet girls danced the *Can-Can* for their sweetbacks. "Oh you want to see the Blue-gum Rest, eh? Hail a cab," he said.

In a few minutes we were in a five-room house on Armour Avenue. The landlady had ten coal black girls, all sizes and weights. Four or five were dancing to a tune I thought was the old college song, *Didn't He Ramble*. One of the visiting students from Yale or Harvard brought it to White Sulphur Springs and used it in one of the school shows. After they finished their sexual dance, to display their efficiency, and the house had a few drinks, I asked the lady on the stool who wrote the parody on *Didn't He Ramble*. You could have knocked my head off with a feather when she told me that the authors of *Didn't He Ramble* stole the theme from the sweetbacks and hotpots of Chicago. It seemed the original song began about an old billy goat that roamed the streets and alleys around Armour Avenue, between South 12th and 31st Street—the heart of the Tenderloin district, where hundreds of men and women earned their living by making love. This old goat, by close association, soon learned that he could do better by joining the profession than he was doing following the garbage-can route he was on. So he did.

The time wasn't long before the men in the district began to envy him. Old Bill used to show up every morning with his goatee combed in a different twist and he rambled all over the place. Finally he got mixed up with a band of goats being driven to the stock yards for slaughter, and he was killed by mistake. The news was quickly spread about the district that old Billy was dead. A jolly crowd was told of his death one night in a brothel. At the end of the story, one man ejaculated with an oath, "That ----- rambled until the butchers cut him down." The ragtime piano-player soon found a tune to fit the phrase. They added a few more words that were not so sweet, and *Didn't He Ramble* was conceived.

She started to play another number about the low-downs on the district, when a sugar-man came in and demanded money from his hotpot to gamble with. She told him of her slow evening. He knocked her clean across the room. She got up and picked up a table lamp and threw it at his head. It struck the wall and burst into flames. The rest of us left the house—my pal and I by the back door. When the fire wagons arrived, we stood among the crowd that watched the fire. We had to laugh to hear the different things said as to how it started. How quick the lies begin! It was three A. M. when I bid him good-night on the corner of 31st and State.

The following day, I was in the station an hour ahead of train time, just long enough to read the railroad pamphlets. The Pennsylvania had listed spots along their route to look out for as mountain beauty. I was surprised to learn they were talking of foot-hills—for that's what they were to me. On an' on, the big Steel Jack snaked the swaying carriages. Harrisburg, Philadelphia—the home of Wm. Penn, whom Mannie Gordon had read of in history. He would have gotten out to see the sights, but Wm. Moran was an experienced man—nothing excited him.

The platform man made my heart pound when he called out "This train for Trenton—Newark—Jersey City and New York." *New York. NEW YORK CITY!* It rang through my head like a death bell ringing in your ear. I lived all my life over again. All of mother's superstitions came to me. Had any black cats crossed before me? Did I turn back for anything? When last did I sweep dust over a door sill at night? Did I spill any salt on the trip? Had I killed a spider, by mistake? Would the seven years bad luck for killing each cat follow me even in New York City? Then there was God I hadn't talked to every night as she had told me to. Would He punish me for that? If all these things were true I hadn't kept much ACCOUNT OF THEM. Would New York City be the place I would have to pay off in full for these spiritual crimes, I wondered?

My first ride up dark Fifth Avenue, at ten P. M. was not much of a thrill to me. I had seen livelier nights, riding on horseback through Dead Man's Gulch, during an electric storm in the dark. William Moran might have been pleased, but he died coming into Jersey City, when the conductor cut his last stub, and I had to pay a few cents to bury him.

The cab stopped at 636 Fifth Avenue. In a few minutes I was face to face again with John Ringling, the king of the BigTop. His wonderful personality swept all fear I might have had into oblivion. I felt assured that no evil would happen to me soon. He put me in the hands of his butler, Ed, a colored man who had been with him for years. Ed gave me a room in the servants' quarters on the roof of the tall apartment house. After I cleaned up, I returned to the kitchen in the apartment, to talk with Ed and Jessie. She was the cook, Ed's wife—a little, short, high brown woman in her forties. With what experience I had had with my people, I found they were as different in ways as they are in colors. Knowing scarcely anything about Negroes, I immediately began to question Ed and Jessie as to the customs of these in New York. They told me they were of many types—all kinds of mixtures, and for me not to think that every brown-skinned person was colored. (I noticed they used the word

COLORED.) Ed said, "They may look colored, but they're not—they might be East Indians or dark South Americans or something else. And white Americans treat them differently. They can eat and sleep wherever they have money enough to pay for it. And you use discretion about starting a conversation with them. They dislike the curly-headed American Negro."

At eleven o'clock, Ed and I walked down to 53rd Street to the old Marshal Hotel, where the Clef Club musicians and big sports met the Broadway actors and actresses. That night made me feel that of all the places I had been, New York was the best.

Ed and I got to bed about two o'clock. I almost talked him to death. The next morning I was up and down for breakfast at eight. It was two hours before Ed had to serve Mrs. Ringling. Mr. Ringling and C. C. Wilson, the guest at the house, didn't have their breakfasts until one P. M. After they were served, Mr. Ringling sent for me to come into the library. He asked me what I had been doing since I had left L. N. Scott. After I told him, he said, "Well, then, you can handle my private car, can't you?" I told him I thought I could. "The car is in the B. & O. yards, Jersey City. Mrs. Ringling will give you a list for food. Get it filled at Summer Brothers' meat market on Sixth Avenue. I'll let you know when we are leaving town."

So I wasn't going to get a chance to see New York at all!

CHAPTER 12

MY FIRST TRIP SOUTH

IN two days' time, I was stocking up Ringling's private car, The Wisconsin, for a trip to Sarasota, Florida. The third day we were coasting into Washington, D. C., behind a B. & O. train. All I saw of the A. B. C. city from the train, as we headed south over the Seaboard Airline, was the tops of government buildings and the great Washington Monument. At that time little did I think that ten years later I would be singing there for one of America's most prominent society leaders, Mrs. Schlesinger, when she entertained international guests in her Capitol City home.

As we ran farther south, going through town after town, it seemed to me someone had lied about the south. No MISCEGENATION down there?! According to western customs, there was nothing *but* mixed marriages. In most every yard I saw black men and white women or vice-versa, working together—nailing up something— a lady on a ladder and a niggah holding it. At home all husbands helped their wives to do the work around the house, unless they were rich, and then you never saw either of them do anything. In a little town in South Carolina, the Jenkins Band of fifteen boys was playing a blaring ragtime number. They were surrounded by more Negroes than I had ever seen at one time before in life. I ran into the front of the car, for Mrs. Ringling and her guests to come and see all the colored people. You should have seen the expression on their faces. In bed that night I laughed when I realized what probably ran through their minds— me calling them to look at colored folks—as black as *I* am!

Yellow clay—yellow clay—muddy rivers—pine trees —ATLANTA—JACKSONVILLE—hot sun—TAMPA—SARASOTA, FLORIDA.

I soon found out that John Ringling and his brothers were big men in Sarasota. Every one knew them as the rich Yankees, and anything or anybody connected with them became RINGLINGS. The day after my arrival, I was known as Ringling's Niggah. Niggah didn't mean anything, but to be a rich man's niggah—that established the amount of liberty the individual niggah was to have. The niggah of a man with a hundred thousand dollars couldn't do what a millionaire's niggah could do . . . Oh! no—not by a long shot.

I spent a couple of days on the car, then on to the beautiful Ringling estate on Sarasota Bay, some five or six miles north of the city. Mr. Ringling and his party did not stay long in Sarasota on that trip—just ten days or so. They returned to New York without me. I stayed in the big house all by myself for nearly two months. During the day, I did light work, preparing things for workmen who were remodeling a part of the house. At night I spent my time studying my people—their ways and actions—what they called PLAY. I took in many of the camp meetings held in the woods. I went to their church meetings, held in their half tumbled-down shacks. It was at these religious gatherings that I saw how mother got the fear of God ground into her soul: it was by dominating characters singing, barking and stomping their belief into susceptible minds, made so by suffering. Old Reverend Colson of Sarasota was an uneducated man of eighty-six years old, but had somehow learned the stories of the Bible and knew how to tell them. By swaying his humped back, throwing his long arms, chopping off his words as if his God was taking his breath, he held his mourners to his belief. Probably if mother had been dead at the time, I might have had a different feeling about the affair. Maybe I would not have gotten the amusement out of joining in on the ring shouts, as I did.

Every colored man in Sarasota had a girl of some sort, even those that had lived years as prisoners in terpentine camps and had eaten so much medicine they were sterile. However, they kept the girls on loose reins, hoping that sometime Fate would be kind to them. I fell in line with their customs. I gained the acquaintance of an Indian brown skin gal, five feet six, weight one hundred and twenty pounds. She lived just across the dead line on the main road to the Ringling estate, in a big brown house with a gray sand yard, the house set up on short pegs. That girl was really a pippin. I used to take her out riding in the boss' car. We were getting along fine when Ringling and his guests returned to Florida.

For a few weeks the Ringling party played and rested

in the southern sun. Fishing was their best pleasure. Nearly every other day, their yachts could be seen leaving Sarasota Bay for the Grouper banks, on a tarpon-fishing trip. I made some of those trips with them as chef. They never swam much, because the sharks were so bad out in front of the Ringling estate in Sarasota Bay. Although swimming was my long suit, I seldom tried it there. Every night they set a bait for sharks out at the dock. The next morning we could see the rope tied at the dock just a-foaming the water, with a shark trying to get away from the big hook. Finally the time came for Mr. C. C. Wilson and Mr. Ringling and I to take a trip north to Chicago in the private car, then back to Florida. Ringling and C. C. went straight to the estate when we returned. I stayed on the car. The next day I was polishing the brass railing around the observation end of the car, when one of the clerks from the grocery store (where Ringlings bought most of their goods) came by.

"Hal-low, Ring-lun. How'as the trip up north? Didja bring any red lick-ker back widjah?" he whined.

"Yes—yah want alittle taste?" I answered.

We boarded the car and went in to the pantry. I opened up a bottle of Old Crow. He poured his own troubles—a good swig, in a high-ball glass. I never did drink much, but I had a little with him to be sociable. He supped half of the drink down, then continued to ask me questions. Alf T. Ringling had brought two West Indian girls (maids) down with him from New York. This fellow wanted to know about them.

"Say, where'd them two gals of ol' Alf T's hail from?" he asked.

"British West Indies," I answered.

"Yah don't say. I kinda thought they hada funny brogue. I'd like to meet that light one, sometime. She's a peach. Say, yahno, I'm goin' upta Tampa, sometime next week. Supposen I bring a jug of red lick-ker, and you hav'em down here on the car some night, and I'll bring Slater down, and we'll have some fun. Hey?" he said.

"That'll be fine—we'll have a double quartet party. You know Sam and I rush those gals every now and then. . . ." (Sam was my pal in Florida, a long, tall, black fellow). "You'll bring a couple of white gals along with you, too, won't you?" I said.

He had started to drink the rest of his whiskey. It had gotten almost to the stomick when I said "white gals". It bolted and came right back up—flew all over me and the pantry. He looked like a man who had been firing a furnace and it bursted. With his mouth wide open, he said "Noop, ba God", and rushed up out of the door, jumped down off the car and disappeared around the corner.

I began to think to myself I shouldn't have said that to him—that he'd get his gang and burn my hinie for that. I finished polishing the little patch on the railing quickly, and prepared to tell Mr. Ringling what had happened. The mob didn't show up as quickly as I thought it should, so I thought to myself that he had gotten over his hot-headedness. I looked all ways for a crowd but found none. I walked up to the colored district kinda uneasy.

The next morning I had to go into the store for a gunny sack for Mr. Ringling (he wanted to go get some King oranges from some orchard). "Say Fletcher, have you got a gunny sack in here? Ringling wants one," I said.

The clerks were putting up orders and no customers were in the place. It was a few seconds before anyone answered. Finally Fletcher, the boss, said from behind the counter. "No, we aint got no gunny sacks."

I looked back by some boxes and one was laying on the floor. "There's one laying there," I said, pointing to it.

"Oh, you mean a crocker sack," Fletcher said.

"Oh, you call them crocker sacks down here?" I asked.

"Say—come here," beckoning for me to come back of the counter. I went.

"Say—where dajah hail from?" he asked.

"Montana," I answered.

"I reckon there aint many niggers up there, is there?" he said.

"Nope, just my family," I said.

"Ahum," he grunted, and shook his head up and down. "Well—ain't the white people up there got any handles to their names?" he asked.

"Sure. Henry, John, Edith," I said.

"Naw, naw! I mean Miss and Mister," he said.

"Oh, yes, but they seldom use 'em," I answered.

"Well, by God! We use 'em down here, and I'd advise

you to get the habit, if you know what's good for yah.
Now take that sack and get out of here," he said.

Some thing told me then that I shouldn't go down
South too many times. I was cutting too many hogs in
Florida.

*　　*　　*

The circus was opening up in Madison Square Garden
in New York City. Mr. Ringling returned for the great
day, and I went with him. After two days' work with
the auto, carrying trunks and small things off of the
private car brought from Florida, I locked it up and
left it in the B. & O. private car yards in Jersey City.
I didn't return to the car until the circus left New York
for the road. I had a room in the servants' quarters on
top of the high apartment house where Ringling lived.
I didn't have much work to do at first in New York. Ed
and Jessie were still with the Ringlings. My duty was
to keep Mr. Ringling's wardrobe in order, valet, all
except shave him. He shaved himself. He said he never
let a barber shave him—they ruined his face. He had a
razor for each day in the week, the old-fashioned kind.
He was a real Beau Brummel in those days, and *particular!* I remember one time he had four dozen shirts made
by a Fifth Avenue shirt shop, and after wearing each
one a coupla times, he didn't like the way they hung
on his left shoulder, and had them all taken back. And
the shirt shop took them! I said to myself, My, what a
break rich folks get! To show my hard luck—I coulda
bought those shirts for a song, but if you took in the
neck, the sleeves would be too short. Ringling wore a

sixteen and a half collar and I wore a fifteen at the time. I never fell heir to any of his clothes, except a necktie once in a while. Someone on his wife's side of the family was that lucky bird, and his shoes were too short for me. As a rule Mr. Ringling would be out of the house by two-thirty or three P. M., and I'd be right out after him. If I had to help do any cleaning in the morning, we were always through before either Mr. or Mrs. Ringling were up, although Mrs. Ringling awoke early nearly every morning.

So most every afternoon and evening, I would go down to the Garden or some other theatre. I learned to tell every act in the circus by their music and I got acquainted with most everyone around the place. It was a great pleasure for me to watch the milling mobs myself. I studied their peculiar ways and actions. The best show of all for me was to see and listen to the people who asked questions of the Freaks, who sold their pictures to them. That was a curious thing to me—people absolutely strangers buying folks' pictures. It should have been even exchange. New York had me guessing if I were sane. To the lady that swallowed the sword they'd ask, "Did it go all the way down the first time you tried it? Is there any taste to it? How many children have you got?" To the fat lady, "Do you dance? Who taught you, the giant?" They were always surprised to learn her husband was one of the dwarfs and then they'd ask, "Why do you prefer little men?" To the tatooed man, after they had turned all around him, "Did brown going in hurt more than blue ink?" To the bearded lady, "Is your hair much bother at night?" And little kids would ask their parents of old Zip, "Mother, has the head always been pointed?"

I thought the Easterners should be the wisest people in the world. They ask enough questions.

One morning while I was putting the buttons in Mr. Ringling's shirt, he told me they were going to leave town with the circus, that they were going as far as Philadelphia, and then that he would leave the show and go West. He gave me orders to get the car in shape, to have the storage batteries and lights overhauled, and stock up heavy with special things like Pilsner beer, Poland Water and White Rock; special foods like Virginia Hams and Summer Brothers' products that could not be bought on the road—also the liquors. I was a week getting ready for my first trip with the circus.

The day we left, the sun was shining bright and the circus train seemed unusually brilliant. Ed and Jessie stayed in New York. Jessie used to cook on the private car, too, but this time I managed the car all by myself—cook, waiter and porter—that was my job all the time I was on the car, except on special occasions, when they had four or five extra guests. Then I had a chef for that special trip.

While the Circus afforded great pleasure to me in New York, I really didn't understand what a great thing it was until we hit the road under the Big Top. Everything worked like clock work. Even the horses that pulled up the tent-poles, knew when a post was in the right position. They would stop by themselves—and how they loved the crowds that watched them at work. The men that put up and down the tents, they are the proudest lot that ever lived. In all of Napoleon's career never did he have a man under him that felt any more honored and loyal than a tent hustler of the Big Top. Between the matinee, or after the night shows, I would go round to see some of every group in the show, shoot crap or play their favorite games of gambling. Lots of sevens and elevens I have seen thrown for weeks' pay.

The circus was hard on the moral code of the ballet girls. One season they had a hundred and fifty girls dancing in the King Solomon spectacle. They had special cars for them, and hours to be in at night. It kept Sam McCracken preaching daily to them. "Please don't be seen leaving hotels in the city in the daytime—it looks so crude." "Do leave the patrons alone on the circus grounds, for the business's respectability." One girl got really unreasonable. Mr. Ringling had to take her in charge. He threatened to pay her off. She told him, "God financed me at birth—don't worry about me," and she bid him farewell in the most unusual words of slang. It made the long black cigar bounce from one side of his mouth to the other, and his eyes battered like a man who had been looking at the eclipse of the sun without smoked glasses.

This little roccous was very interesting to me, because it was the first time I had heard my new boss reprimand anyone, and I considered myself lucky that the young lady talked back. It gave me a chance to study the points of the great man's character which it might fall on me to be tackfull with.

Everything about the big show thrilled me from putting up the tents to selling the tickets. I think the sweetest graft of all is held by the men on the ticket boxes selling the paste-boards. People at a circus seldom count their change, lots of them go away and leave it all behind, and on the Freak Show it's a crime the way they get upset. There is something about the word Freak that affects the public's mind.

John Ringling never stayed with the show for more than three weeks at a time when I was with him. We would go off to some other place on business. Many a trip was made to Oklahoma, where he built a railroad and developed an oil field. I knew Oklahoma was dry like most southern states were at the time, so people there must be wild about Red Lick-ker. In St. Louis I filled all my possom boxes with Red Lick-ker. I felt that if anything would save a Niggah in the south, it would be to give the bosses of the town Red Lick-ker when first I met them, so they'd mark me as a good nigger. Then they'd tell the ruffians to lay off me.

I won honor in Ardmore, Oklahoma, for sure. Any other spade would have gotten burned for what happened. Ringling's car was backed up so he could step to the street quickly on Ardmore Avenue. The kitchen end of the car was nearest to the walk, so people couldn't look into the rich man's parlor. You could hear the conversation between Jack Grear and I from the sidewalk when you passed. (Jack was a special cook for the occasion.)

There was a white woman who had about fifteen or twenty cheap gingham dresses, all shades and cuts. She went downtown a dozen times a day and each time she went in a new dress, carrying a little red parasol for a sunshade. The way she stepped you could tell she hated herself. Jack had been up in the colored section and he had vamped two browns. Every night he'd go out with them. I was sick and needed plenty rest, so I stayed on the car. In the mornings he would tell me what was done the night before. It was his luck to be saying, "Man, she's a peach," speaking of the brown, when this white woman was going downtown past the car. She misunderstood him.

That evening as I was serving the cocktails for dinner, who stepped up on the car, but the sheriff and his deputy. They greeted me politely as they entered. You could have picked out my eyes with a pair of boxing gloves on when I found out they were there to lock Jack and me up for insulting this woman. If it hadn't been for the Red Lik-ker and Mabel Ringling overhearing part of the same conversation between Jack and I—Oklahomians might have had some teeth and toe-nail souveniers of a Yankee Niggah. I ordered the car moved that night. Never would another hot sunlight show us that dress parade again.

Months later two workmen were fixing a leaking gasoline railroad tank car. They struck a spark with a hammer, the tank blew up, and all the buildings around the

station in Ardmore were knocked down. Over fifty people were killed including that woman. Look up my coat
sleeve.

* * *

The next week found C. C. Wilson and J. R. and
his car in Houston, Texas. They left the car for business. I cleaned up, put on my new Jack Johnson plaid
suit, patent leather shoes, hotcap to see Houston.
Through the station I started, looking at the old confederate pictures of great southern generals. Right in the
center of the station, on the north wall, was a big picture of Stonewall Jackson or General Lee, I can't remember which. The confederate colors were crossed
above it. I was reading the history on the copper plate
under it, when someone grabbed my coat lapel, twisting
it all up. I grabbed the hand and jerked it off, with the
remark, "Don't twist my clothes like that." As I turned,
my eyes fell on a man dressed in a gray civilian suit,
slouch Stetson hat, with a big star, nearly six inches
across, on his left breast. He had a two and a half billy-
club in his hand.

"Damn you! I'll twist your head—what you doin' in
here? You're a Yankee Nigger, ain't cha?" he said.

Intuition told me I was in dutch. "No, I'm Ringling's
Niggah," I said.

"Oh, you don't say. Well, by God! that saves yah.
You sure look like a Yankee Nigger. They're all too
damn smart. At any rate you can't come in here with
those clothes on. Come here and I'll show you where
Niggers belong," he said.

He ushered me out the front door of the station, around the north corner, and showed me a kind of rain shed, with a few benches along the wall.

"There's where you belong in them clothes. If you want to see the sights in that station, put on your uniform," he said.

I went back to the car and put on my white coat, duck pants, red porter's cap with SARASOTA in gold letters all across the front. Then I went out to see Houston, Texas.

The Ethiopians of the district were having their annual Fish Fry. Also, the circus was in town. The darkeys came from far and near, the laboring class. No society spades would think of attending a Fish Fry themselves; they'd send some boy to stand where they knew, by some means, that the cook put a wicked brown on a catfish, for an order to eat at home. I was told, of all the sights to see, don't miss the Fish Fry. They directed me down to the railroad track, where I crossed and walked a few blocks west to a vacant lot. The colored people had this lot covered with tents, cook stoves of all kinds, charcoal pots and campfires—all with some kind of a kettle of hot grease on them, frying fish. The customers were like a big black mass of moving ants, when you step on their hill accidentally. Out on a little green spot, a man and woman were lying on the ground, eating fish offa spread-out newspaper with their hands. stood near them and heard this conversation:

Man: This fish sho is good.

Woman: Ain't they.

Man: I wonder who first named the fish, "Fish".
(Time was past for swallowing.)

Woman: Christ named the fish, "Fish".

Man: How come no one ever *talked* with Christ?

Woman: Yes, they did. The day Christ named the fish, "Fish", He fed a whole town of people, as big as Houston, on one fish.

Man: On *one* fish? Stop your kidding! It musta been a whopper. . . . I've heard tell of fish as big as whales, but they don't eat 'em.

Woman: No, this wasn't a big fish. Christ held it in his hand: I saw the picture of it.

Man: A SEASONED FISH, huh?

Woman: I ain't never heared of a SEASONED FISH.

Man: Hush yo mouth. You've eaten many seasoned fish. You see, you put a salt on this fish because it comes from the clear water, but seasoned fish comes from the ocean and they don't need any salt on them.

Woman: Oh, I guess you is right.

Man: Christ sho knowed his stuff—feed all them people on one seasoned fish. One mouthful, then they fill up on water! Ha-ha-ha-hee!

Woman: Ain't it the truth.

Man: Den Christ made the salt, too—huh?

Woman: Cos he did.

Man: I forgives my elder den, and I'se gwine back to the church again, fore dere's nothing I likes better than SALT PORK, CORN BEEF and SEASONED FISH!

And the conversation ended in laughter. I could hear

them laughing as I left the lot. There was no way for the man to stick the woman on any questions about Christ. She had lived as intimately with him as Esther Murphy has lived with Napoleon-Josephine and George Washington.

*   *   *

The next day we were on our way to New Orleans, the city of love. I mean where you go to learn how to make love. The boring trip between Texas and Mississippi into Louisiana, was made much pleasanter to me by that thought alone. Every once in a while the porter in the Pullman car ahead of us would run back and tell me to look out of the window in different towns and see the amusing signs, like: "NIGGER—READ AND RUN", "NIGGER—DON'T LET THE SUN GO DOWN ON YOU HERE", "NIGGERS AND DOGS NOT ALLOWED". That last one made me feel very, very remorseful. I was a murderer of my kin. One day a dog ran in front of the car I was driving and he was killed.

The sudden stopping of the train knocked me out of my sad dreams. Newsboys were calling the New Orleans papers. Ringling and his guest hastened off the hot car. I was soon dressed for the street, in my Jack Johnson plaid, just the thing to have at that time. I had talked so much to the porter in the pullman car ahead of us going to New Orleans about the school where you learn how to make love, he said he'd take me to it, if I would meet him at ten P. M. in the station. We walked about the town, saw a few sights, bought some souveniers, then returned to the private car. We had a few drinks to steady our nerves and then we set off for Madam D'Mounteous, a school for the art of making love.

The doorbell was answered by a little round-faced high-brown servant girl, dressed in a black dress with a white apron about the size of a lady's handkerchief on. There was a little lace cap pinned on the front of her bushy reddish hair. Into the parlor we were asked to have seats. The maid's broken French or broken English, I don't know which, was fascinating and snaring to us.

The Madam came in to the parlor dressed in a long lace gown. She was about five feet ten inches tall with an old cream-yellow complexion, jet black nearly straight hair, with sharp features, kinda Bostonish. She had the most soft looking big brown eyes. The gown she wore gave one the impression that she had just gotten out of bed in her red nightgown, and put a black lace overcoat on over it, buttoning up the front, to attend to business in her office, the latter being her parlor. Harris and I stood as she came toward us with her hands outstretched to greet us. "Oh, so you two came to learn how to make ze love, what?" she said with her French accent.

We both grinned and giggled "he, he," then answered "yes," like it had been rehearsed. "Well, make yourselves at home, in a moment I will send in ze teachers so you may see them for yourselves. I will make ze business arrangement with you," she said and left the room.

She had hardly gotten out of the room before the

maid returned with a tray full of drinks and passed them to us. As we started to drink, two girls came in to the parlor. They were very young, not over twenty. They were attired in cool looking silk gowns and walked with a rolling stride. The tall one resembled the madam, I thought she was her daughter. The other one was a few inches shorter and somewhat darker in complexion with a plump figure.

"Ah, strangers to New Orleans, no? We hope, yes, because it is much nicer to teach strangers than people around here in New Orleans. Oh, it requires all of one's skill to teach them, what, No-Nonette?" the tall one said, putting the question to us and swinging sideways to No-Nonette for the answer, who stood a little back of her to the left. No-Nonette agreed with her, then the tall one continued to talk. "My name is Isucaleana Seengle. Meet my dear collaborator, No-Nonette Pvaslyne. I'm sorry her sister is not teaching today. She is very charming, but not so nice as Nonette—no?" she said, and pulled Nonette's cheeks.

Harris and I mumbled out our first names and then they asked us to be seated again. I sat on the divan. Harris took a straight backed chair. The room we were in had a long sideboard cabinet in it. You could see the dishes and eating utensils inside of the glass doors. There was a large round table and a few other pieces of furniture, not many, setting about. It was one of those kind of decorated rooms that puzzles your mind as to whether it is the parlor or the dining room and you come to the conclusion that the occupants of the house use it for both.

Not many words were passed between us before the madam returned again. "Well, gentlemen, these are the only teachers at liberty at the present. Do they suit your fancies—yes?" She had answered for us, so we nodded our heads to O. K. her spoken approval. "Then they will give you your first lesson in making ze love. Ze fee is five dollars each an hour, is that satisfactory—no?" she asked, but held her hand out for the money. Our answer was putting the cash into her hands as she stepped toward us with a theatrical smile on her face, head held slanting off to the right side, sort of posing like. She took the green-backs and held them up to the light to see if they were good. After the money had passed her inspection, "Nice gentlemen, give them all the fine points, girls—you understand," she said, with a more Frenchy accent, and left the room.

"Have you ever had any lessons at making love before?" Isucaleana asked me.

I had learned never to tell any teacher you knew anything if you wanted to get the best results, so I said no. "Well, then I will start from the beginning," she said, as she sat down on the divan beside me. Her first instructions dwelled upon the essential parts of the human anatomy one must know about if they wanted to be successful in love making. Next she told me how different people were in manners and styles, but there were a few things in common with the majority, and the minor proportion could easily be persuaded, if the love-maker was efficient in his art. Then followed the *do's* and *don't's* unless you couldn't help it; and if you did by chance do the wrong thing to always make up in some other fashion. She tried to explain how to find out if one loved you. That was a long chapter and I can't remember anything about it, except if you have been keeping company with a young lady for a long time and you had been used to giving her loads of presents, as well as seeing that she saw most of the new shows, then suddenly you stopped because of financial conditions and the girl did not quit you—that was a sign she really loved you. She also said it was always better not to give anything at all unless you could give what they wanted, never to kiss anyone with tight lips, and good teeth were the most alluring thing to women—a stubby mustache the most obnoxious. Isucaleana demonstrated everything that required action to make clear.

Harris and Nonette came back into the parlor: they had been in the study looking at some text books. Harris sat down on the same straight back chair. Nonette sat on his lap. Some cigarettes had been passed. Isucaleana struck a match on her heel, then laid back across my lap and lit the cigarette in my mouth. Nonette saw this done and must have thought she had to do something attractive too. "Oh, I can light my pupil's cigarette too," she said. Her black eyes flashed with egotism. Then she leaned back like a contortionist, lit a match on her slipper with her legs wrapped around Harris' lap, chair and all. Harris had on a wing celluloid collar. When Nonette straightened up, she tried to put her arm around Harris's neck to light the cigarette. Somehow she slipped a little and the match lit the end of that celluloid collar. It flared up *vit-vit-ziss*, like half-damp gunpowder. Isucaleana jumped up, grabbed a pail half full of stale drinks, beer-corks and cigarette stubs, throwing them on Harris's head before Nonette could get up, she was so shocked. The cure was worse than the fire. The flame singed Harris's hair and burnt his neck so much that we had to discontinue the lesson.

CHAPTER 13

BACK TO FLORIDA

THE latter part of the week, Ringling was back in Sarasota again for a short stay. I knew I wouldn't be able to be back in Florida soon again, so I decided to give all the time I could to the copper-colored brown, who lived in the big house across the line. Remember her? I took her out nightly. One Monday morning I got a letter showing a sketched picture of an automobile dangling by its hind wheels off a bridge, and a Niggah hanging to a tree off the side of the creek. At the bottom was written:

IF YOU DON'T LET THAT GAL ALONE THIS WILL BE A PICTURE OF YOU.

It puzzled me a great deal. I said to myself, "Damn! Have I been flirting with any white gals in Florida?"

I began to case every gal and woman I knew in the town. I couldn't place anyone I had been so fly with so much as I should be hanged about. So I showed the note to Sam, my buddie.

"I know that writing; I used to take notes for him—it's the clerk in the bank," he said.

"Clerk in the bank, Hell! I ain't going with his gal, am I? You ain't never seen me with any white gals out of line, have you?" I asked.

"No, she ain't white—that Emma is his gal on the

QT. All these peckerwoods runs around with these black gals when they can git 'em," he said.

I took the letter to John Ringling. He is sure one ofay man that didn't find an alibi to get in line with the peckerwoods. He went to town and caught a mob of thirty or more young fellows standing in front of the barber shop, their evenings' hang-out. The young clerk was with them. Ringling cussed them for all he was worth, called them every low-down word he could think of and told them he'd burn the damn town down if they touched me. After that, when the gang saw me, they would holler at me clear across the street, "Hallow, Ringlun."

They informed anyone that didn't know me that I was Ringlun's nigger and to lay off me. I said to myself, whata hell ofa country for me. I can't *look* at a white woman, and they'll kill me for entertaining a brown one. So every year after that I found the blackest gal in Sarasota for my company and Sam told me I wasn't safe even with her.

* * *

IN THE SUMMER OF 1915

It was in the summer of 1915 that John Ringling's private car was backed up to the sidewalk in the private car-yards at St. Louis, Mo. The weather was grand. A breeze was floating slowly through the open windows. No one was on the car but me. I had finished cleaning up everything and had the victrola playing a record of Enrico Caruso's *Pagliacci*. I was chiming in with it to amuse myself. I imagined that I was singing the role on the Metropolitan stage, as I had seen Caruso do many times when I was in New York. When the record was finished someone stepped up on the observation platform, and peeked through the screen door.

"Who's singing in here? You?" the man asked.

"No, Caruso. Ha ha!" I said.

"Yes, I know it was a Caruso record, but who was singing with it?" he asked.

"Me. Why?" I said.

"Well, you've got a good voice and should study. Where do you live?" he asked.

"I'm Ringling's private man. We travel all over, but New York is his headquarters," I said.

"That's fine. I'll give you my friend's address. He's looking for talent. When you get to New York go to see him; maybe he can use you," he said.

He wrote a note to Max Bendix on the back of his card and left the card before I could thank him good. I put the card in my address book and didn't give it much thought. I had never given music any consideration for a profession. Everyone else in the family could sing or play on some kind of instrument but me. The only singing I ever did was in school. I heard so much of it at home it really bored me.

Just as I started to go into the street, Charlie Kennally, Ringling's private secretary, came on the car. I told him what had happened. He said Max Bendix was a great musician in New York City and if I could get him to handle me I would be a lucky man. Kennally always advised me to study music. His mission to the car at that hour was to tell me Mr. Ringling was leaving for Chicago that night. I had to hustle for food to make the trip. I didn't have any fresh eggs or lamb kidneys, fruit or any of Mr. Ringling's favorite breakfast dishes, on account of the hot weather.

In three hours' time, we were hooked on the tail end of a crack train, north bound. The following morning, we were in Chicago. Every railroad company always allowed him to leave his car in the station as long as he cared to leave it there, but as a rule, he left the car soon after the train that it was hooked on to hit the town where he was going. In all the small towns, and with the circus, he slept on the car—also in the southwest, like Oklahoma and Texas. We stayed in Chicago for a few days and Mrs. Ringling joined us. From there, we went west to Montana. It was the first time I had been home since I had left, nearly five years before. To the folks at home, I was the berries. I had already been farther and seen more towns than any six people in White Sulphur had seen together in their lives.

John Ringling had bought the old Parbery house, the big mansion on the west end of Main Street, south side. There were only two big houses in that part of town. It was about two blocks from the railroad station.

After they got settled in the big house, my duty kinda shifted to yard man and chauffeur. Ed and Jessie had quit in New York. I think they had been with the

Taylor Gordon. Photograph by Carl Van Vechten. (Beinecke Library, Yale University Library)

Taylor Gordon's brothers and sister. *Top:* (left) Robert James, (right) George Wellington; *bottom:* (left) John Francis Jr., (right) Rose Beatris; (E. Taylor Gordon Collection, Montana Historical Society)

Top: Mary Ann Gordon (1853–1924), mother of Taylor Gordon. *Bottom:* Taylor Gordon, 1919. (E. Taylor Gordon Collection, Montana Historical Society)

Top: J. Rosamond Johnson at piano; Taylor Gordon standing *Bottom:* (left to right) Edward Ransom, Taylor Gordon, Pete Za brisky, and J. Rosamond Johnson, 1919, New York City. (E. Taylor Gordon Collection, Montana Historical Society)

Taylor Gordon. Photograph by Carl Van Vechten. (J. W. Johnson Collection, Beinecke Library, Yale University Library)

Taylor Gordon, Helena, Montana, April 1936. Taken after Gordon had been snowbound for the winter. (J. W. Johnson Collection, Beinecke Library, Yale University Library)

Top: Taylor ("Manny") Gordon with teacher and classmates in White Sulphur Springs, Montana. (E. Taylor Gordon Collection, Montana Historical Society). *Bottom:* White Sulphur Springs, Montana. (E. Taylor Gordon Collection, Montana Historical Society)

Taylor Gordon, 1968. (E. Taylor Gordon Collection, Montana Historical Society)

Ringlings nearly twenty years. The servants they had out west were New York Swedes and Irish women. I didn't have much to do in the house unless it was mechanical work to be done.

Oh, yes! I had to milk the cow out there at that time, too. One day I mowed the lawn and stacked the grass all up in the back lot. The kind hearted old Swedish housekeeper thought it would be nice to let the cow have it, so she opened the gate and let this full-blooded Jersey cow eat the grass. That night, when I went to milk the cow (I always milked her in the field) she wouldn't stand still. I noticed she was in agony. Finally I got her milked, after tying her up. Then I took the milk into the kitchen and left it with the cook. When I came out of the kitchen door, I noticed all of the green grass had been moved. I asked the cook who took the grass. She told me Hilda, the housekeeper, let the cow eat it. Mr. Ringling was told of the coincidence, and Charlie White, the veterinary doctor, a kid I went to school with, was called. He gave her a few big white pills and left her in the corral that night. The next morning at eight o'clock, when I went to see how she was, I found her stretched out in the shed, gasping for breath. Doc White came up on his saddle horse a few minutes after I got there. I helped him perform an operation on the cow. We cut her paunch open and took most of the grass out, and sewed her up, and in a few hours the cow got up. They took her to the Catlan's farm, a ranch Ringling had bought, between Dorsey and White Sulphur. It was the only farm with a private fishing lake on it in the county. When I was a kid, we used to steal out there and fish every once in a while. We caught big salmon trout about twelve to twenty inches long. It was also a great place to shoot ducks and geese. The first goose I ever killed in my life, I killed out there.

I was glad to see my people, as they were to see me. I asked Mother why she didn't tell me how colored people were treated in the South. She cried, and told me she had tried to keep me at home, and if we children didn't see ourselves she would never tell any of us about it. She begged me not to go South any more; she was afraid I'd get killed. But I put a knowing bluff on, and told her I knew how to handle Southerners—not to worry. At the same time, I knew what she was talking about was right. I spent a few days with my old friend of the hills, Mr. C. H., and I talked his wife to death about her old birth-place, New York. The way the gang hung around me at nights in the pool-room and listened to my tales, I thought I was Herbert H. Metzger, and was surprised to find myself out of jail.

On that trip out west, Ringling had a new private secretary, a fellow from one of the Carolinas (he had by some means got Kennally canned in New York) I can't remember his name. Everyone loathed him but Mr. and Mrs. Ringling, even C. C. Wilson—and at that time he was almost Mr. Ringling himself. This guy couldn't understand how the people in White Sulphur Springs could treat me as they did. He never did say anything to me personally about Niggahs, but I could tell by his conversation what he thought of them, and me particularly. Every girl and boy that I went to school with that was still in White Sulphur came down on the car. They said to see me, but I think their curiosity as to how the inside of Ringling's car looked was their biggest attraction. Sometimes they'd be boys and girls (a few of the kids had married) and sometimes they'd be just a gang of girls. That kind of a combination always got the gallant young man's goat from the tarheel state. He had a nose that could smell two girls going into the car from the house. No sooner would they get on the car than he'd come arunning over from the house to take the job of telling them about the car, and its workings. It was sometime before I got wise to his idea.

One day two pretty girls came over to the car, and he came on a dog-trot from the house. I told the girls I was not going to introduce him to them, that I wanted to watch his actions. The screen door wasn't hooked, but he rang the bell just the same. I didn't answer it. He came into the dining-room and asked why I didn't answer the bell. I told him I was talking to two ladies. He grinned and looked for an introduction, but I began to ask the girls of school kids we played with, and we ignored him absolutely. He turned red as a beet and walked out. I watched him walk back to the house. The girls had a good laugh and they left.

I forgot it for the time, but it stopped him from butting in while I was in White Sulphur. Soon after that, he never had anything to say to me unless it was nasty—

something that he'd heard Mr. or Mrs. Ringling say
about me. One day I was mowing the lawn: he came to
me and said, "That cow died, and Mrs. Ringling is
going to have Mr. Ringling make you pay for it, but
don't say that I said it." When he said, "Don't say that
I said it," I knew then and there something was wrong
with him, as far as I was concerned. I had been stung
before for saying So-and-so said so, and I'd prove it by
them. When I got So-and-so before the judge, they always said, "Oh, no! You misunderstood me. I said *this*"
and *this* was what always put me in Dutch. So I didn't
say anything to Mr. Ringling. I said to myself I'll
watch what they do with my pay. I never found it cut,
so I made up my mind to make that guy trick himself.

The time came for the Ringling caravan to leave the
golden West. Mrs. Ringling left us at Chicago. She went
to her home in Columbus, Ohio. Mr. Ringling, Fred
Loomis and C. C. Wilson stayed on the car, and we
all joined the circus at Omaha. From there, we went to
St. Paul and Minneapolis, my old stomping grounds.
The Scotts were glad to see all of us, and I was glad
to see them. I had a chat with Mrs. L. N., and she asked
me when I was going to get married. She told me I had
a good position, and I should get married soon. I told her
my same old story about having not enough money, and
decided I was too young. Maybe, when I get to be
thirty-five or forty, if I had enough money; otherwise,
never.

That night, just before the circus started, I was standing on the lot. I saw two girls in the crowd, looking

as if they were lonely. I had had enough experience to know how to crash a circus party, so I did. Both of the girls were very fair. One of the girls was almost questionable. I succeeded in having the opportunity of showing the circus to them. I could always pass at the gate. They never bothered me. I saw Ringling and Fred Loomis watching me going in, and when I got down to the vacant section, just before we sat down, here comes Loomis with an armful of peanuts for us. I wondered if Ringling had sent him, or if he had come on his own hook. I never did find out. I noticed he didn't look at me or the brown. He satisfied himself as to what kind of a woman the light one was. I had satisfied myself that the keen brown would do me for life. She set my mind awhirling. I fell in love with this girl. She was too sweet, and had the most marvellous disposition toward me; everything she did set me giddy. We corresponded daily for about three months. I got my letter, or letters, the same as I got my breakfast. There were times I couldn't eat. I didn't know whether it was the hot weather, or the heat in the kitchen, or the heat in my head for her.

I saved up every dollar I could rake and scrape. I made up my mind to make that sweet woman marry me without thousands of dollars. The week before we pulled into Louisville, Kentucky, I bought a new suit, patent leather shoes—I ragged myself up the best I knew how. I was on the circus by myself. I said, "Umph! Ain't I playin' in luck?"

I thought I'd surprise the young lady by rolling up

to her house in a big car, but it was I that got surprised. When I rang the doorbell and presented my card for her, her mother said, "Why—Bessie has gone to New York *with* the baby. . . ." I learned she had been married nearly two years when I met her, and she had got a kick out of stringing me along. It was some time before I got over that, and I made up my mind then, for sure, I'd never get married without plenty of money.

The circus twined its way on down to Atlanta, Georgia, where they had the biggest day of the season. The box-office pulled $24,000. We were in town two days, Sunday and Monday. The private secretary joined us on Sunday night. He had been to his home up in Carolina, visiting his people. That night when he came on the car he had a lot of smart talk for me. I guess he thought he had me down south and he'd tell me where my place was. He started to tell me how Mrs. J. R. loathed me, and my days were short. I didn't say anything except that I guess it would be all for the best, seeing as he was in so solid as he told me he was.

He was crazy about German Pilsner beer, and every once in a while I'd catch him taking a bottle out of the ice-box. In Montana I gave him sam hill in a nice way, and told him Mr. Ringling couldn't get any more of it from Germany on account of the war. He told me that Ringling didn't care, that anything he did was O. K. with him. I said to myself, how the devil did this guy get the cross on John Ringling in such a short time, when Kennally had been with him for years and couldn't do it, and he always told me I could drink anything but his Pilsner beer.

We were sitting in the dining room, with the plush tablecover on the table. He had helped himself to a cold bottle of German beer, and was setting on the big divan drinking it as he sprung the good news to me. I was hinkty as hell for more than one reason. First, I had been bilked by the gal I was in love with. Second, cause I was down South, and third, cause I loathed him—I loathed the sight of him. My mind was working overtime. I was trying to think how I could trick that guy. He set the empty bottle and glass nearly in the center of the dining-room table, on the plush cloth, and bid me good-night. He slept in the front room, in the next room to the observation end of the car. Something told me John Ringling would be in town on the six A. M. train. Leave that bottle and glass right there, and see what he'd say when he saw it. I did.

The next morning I was up at five, getting breakfast ready for Mrs. Ringling. He only ate two meals a day, and they were two *meals*, I mean: seldom he ever ate anything at that hour in the morning. But Mrs. Ringling could always stand her light breakfast. I was fixing sweetbreads on toast for her when he rang the front doorbell. Mrs. Ringling was with him. I answered it and hustled the baggage on the car. After the usual jolly greeting (I was kinda hinkty and thought to myself, a fine, deceitful lot, getting ready to can me and not telling me anything about it until the time came) Mrs. Ringling went into her room. John sat down in the opposite observation end and asked for the maps. He had a dozen big books of maps, three feet square, of each state and their railroads. Something had happened on the route and it had to be changed. (He routed the show, and Charlie Ringling usually ran it, and stayed with the show most of the season.) I gave him the maps and returned to the kitchen. Then I thought, how the hell would I get him to see that empty bottle? The idea came to me to disconnect the bell so that if he wanted me he'd have to come after me. That worked fine.

In a few minutes he came to the kitchen and said, "Who had the beer?"

"Beer? What beer?" I said.

"The Pilsner. The empty bottle's in on the table," he said.

"Oh, the private secretary had it. He said you didn't care," I said.

"He did, did he? . . . What's the matter with the bell? It don't ring. Mrs. Ringling is ready to eat," he said and walked into the front of the car.

It was hot in the kitchen, and I thought he was leaving on account of the heat. I jumped into service and set up the table quickly. I had everything cooked, and in fifteen minutes she was eating. The secretary rang for breakfast about ten A. M. I served him and said nothing about Ringling, because I couldn't tell whether he was pleased or not, the way he said, "He did, did he?" . . . At any rate, when we left Atlanta, old Sec was not with us. And the rest of the summer I spent in peace.

We made a couple of trips back to Ardmore, and then back to the show. By the middle of November, we were back in New York City. I took the private car to Bridgeport, Conn., the Barnum and Bailey winter headquarters (at that time), then I returned to New York City.

During the summer months of travelling, I lost the card the gentleman gave me, but I remembered the name of Max Bendix. One morning while reading the paper over coffee and toast, I saw an article where Max Bendix was looking for talent to train. His studio was on Madison Avenue at Fiftieth Street. I can't remember the number.

I went over. He had a room full of little children from eight to fourteen years old. Most of them were dressed in ballet dresses and shoes. He had me wait a few minutes, then he tried my voice. I didn't know one note from another, but at any rate he took me up the scale. "Yes, you've got a good baritone voice but you are not a child. I only want children. I'll give you my friend's address; he knows lots of teachers that can help you," he said. He gave me the address of Otto Bartik, the Ballet Master of the Metropolitan Opera House.

I went to him two days later. He took me to a friend of his, who tried my voice. They decided I had a tenor voice of good quality, but I must study at least five years in Italy, and it would cost not less than ten thousand dollars. The following morning while I was putting on Mr. Ringling's shoes, I told him what Bartik said. Ringling and Bartik were good friends. "Ten thousand dollars! My God, that's a lot of money. What do you want to sing for, when you can cook sautéd kidneys so well? Are you getting tired of your job?" he said.

"No, but they say I can earn lots of money by singing if I learn how. I got the main part—the voice," I said.

"I'm late now, I'll think it over," he said.

In a few moments he was going down the elevator. Three days later I popped the question to him again. "Why go to Italy?—Jesus!—most of the European teachers are in New York now, where they can get the money. That music game is a hard game, you know. You go up to the New York School of Music on Seventy-second Street, and if they say you've got a good voice, I'll pay for the lessons," he said.

They received me at the school for voice trial. The place was packed with men and women. Two men and one woman, a pianist, took me into a private room and heard my voice. One man, the manager, left the room for some twenty minutes; then he returned.

"You've got a good voice, but we have a lot of southern pupils here that object to studying with you. We can send you a private teacher," he said.

When Mr. Ringling heard the verdict, "Oh, that's the bunk! You haven't got a good voice. They've got some poor teacher they want to give a few extra dollars to—forget it," he said.

I did until that night. I went down to the Hotel's barber shop on Fifty-third Street to get my hair cut. The shop was full of big-timers from the Clef Club, getting

their hair cut and straightened, and we fell into a conversation about music. They invited me to come to their
rehearsal the following afternoon. Will Marion Cook
was getting ready to direct the *Rain Song* at the Manhattan Casino for the Clef Club rally. Hart, the barber,
told me if I expected to be a big-timer I must have my
hair straightened. So I did. At that time they were using
KINK NO MORE, one dollar and fifty cents a treatment. The stuff burnt my head so I couldn't comb my
hair for a month, and before I could get it cut off, it
turned a burnt red. I looked like a wild man from
Borneo.

I had never sung with any group since school days
when we all sang in unison. The Clef Club men knew
Cook's music backwards, and we were sailing along fine
until I got up on a high note and forgot to come down.
Cook turned into a wild man—pulled his hair, stomped
and cussed all over the place. He frightened me to death.
I got my hat and coat and started out the door. The
last words I heard him say were, "No man can be a
niggah if he sings my music wrong." Ringling's words
were right to me. Music is a tough game.

Sometime later I was leaving the Winter Gardens for
home, musically inspired from seeing and hearing a fine
show. As I turned the corner of Fiftieth Street, the man
running the subway news-stand was putting up a *Musical
Courier* on a display hanger. I bought one. It had hundreds
of teacher ads in it. I picked out Signor Uribee from
Mexico and went to see him. His studio was on 72nd
street. He told me his price was ten dollars a lesson, but he

would teach me for nothing if he could share half of all the money I earned from singing. He said he would take me to South America and to Mexico—if they ever stopped fighting there—then to Europe. Kennally had told me something about that kind of a contract with teachers and to never make one. I hedged on the fifty-fifty proposition. Then he said he would take me as a pupil if I would take a lesson every day at five dollars a lesson, paying for ten lessons in advance. That was my choice. When I had taken nine lessons from him, some of his people got killed in Mexico and he went away.

It was time for Ringling to go South again. In Florida I used to go out on Ringling's yacht when everyone was ashore and practise singing the scales while I played them on a little yacht-organ. It was a difficult thing to do because the little organ had to be pumped so fast to make it sound; but it got me used to singing with an instrument for the first time in my life. Musical instruments with me at first didn't agree. It always sounded a fifth higher to me. I learned a couple of popular hits of the time and I sang them one Saturday night in a little show the waiters and cooks put on in the colored section. Three or four times after that I went with a bunch of men that were good singers of spirituals and southern work-songs to the homes of rich people from the North wintering in Sarasota. As a rule we sang for them out in the Gardens. We were paid by passing the hat. Sometime we split from twenty-five to fifty dollars each night.

Two days after St. Patrick's day, Ringling was on

his way to New York City where the circus was opening up in Madison Square Garden for the season. My regular New York routine began again. The first week I was back I went into Hart's barber shop for a hair-cut, and while I was there Will Marion Cook came and sat in the vacant chair next to me. He recognized me by my speaking voice as the man who ran out of his rehearsal. He was in fine mood and told me to quit my job, that no man with a voice like mine should be a cook. For that reason I quit the great circus-man in New York City.

During the years I spent studying his ways that I might please in his service, I learned many good and few bad things one may use in this life. John Ringling is a man that should live to reach the ripest age of any of the brothers, although none of them I knew got their three-score and ten mark they say every man is allotted. John takes minute care of his health under the instruction of New York's ablest doctors. It is surprising how much he knows about the world, yet seldom you catch him reading any books. He has no special hours for rest. If it takes ten to twenty hours to get the sleep out of his body, he would lay in bed until it's gone. In telling good jokes he is an expert, and his guests always seemed to enjoy his company. I must say I think he was the hardest loser in Pinochle I have ever seen. Whenever his wife and C. C. Wilson could beat him in a game, he would lecture all through the dinner course about how badly they played the game. He always accused them of being too careless in the art, and that was why he lost a few cents. I have never known him to play any of the games of sport like golf or hand ball, and he didn't ride horseback. He was a great outdoors walker, and the average person would almost have to dogtrot to keep up with him in the country. In his home, stiff-legged, bending his six-foot frame until he lays the palms of his hands on the floor, was his main exercise. John Ringling is probably a very pious man, because during all the time I was with him, I never knew him to attend church, or did I catch him praying. A self made rich man who sings in his bath has lived a clean life. All in all, he was a fine man; a little covetous, perhaps, but we all have our idiosyncracies. I might never have left him if Will Marion Cook hadn't of filled my head with the music idea.

Will Cook was living in Harlem at the time with Solomon Johnson, United States Immigrant Inspector. I was to get a job in New York City and study with Cook. You may not believe it, but I walked and rode all over New York City looking for work. Every place I went there would be from ten to twenty men looking for the same job. One evening at dinner, Mrs. Johnson, Solomon's wife, suggested that I buy a job. I went down on Sixth Avenue to the hundreds of employment agencies. They took my money and sent me to jobs that were always just filled before I got there. When I would return for my money, the agent would say that they kept the money, but I'd have a job sure, in a few days. I'd go back when they told me to come back, and they'd have a job for me out of town. Then we'd have an argument—a big argument. They would say, "Well, I got you a job and you don't want it, and now you want your money back. Get the hell out of here. We don't give any money back."

I got stung a few times, then I saw an ad in front of an agency for a chauffeur on Park Avenue for sixteen dollars. I went up to buy it, but when I insisted that the man put on my receipt that if I didn't get the job he'd give me my money back, he give me the same old song, "If you don't get that job, I'll get you some job for the same amount of money." I walked out and never bothered any more agents.

Next I tried putting a chauffeur's ad in the paper. I got three answers for it, one from Long Island, one from Jersey and one from Eighty-sixth Street and River-side Drive. I went to the Eighty-sixth Street apartment house at the time set by the letter to be there. And, by Doctors! there were twenty fellows there, all with the same kind of a letter. We were all to be interviewed and the lucky guy would get a letter the next day, telling him he was employed. We were all reviewed in the parlor, sepa-rately. The madam, a woman around fifty-five with a large bust, dressed in a dark blue lace dress, sat in a big plush chair beside the long library table, and looked at us through glasses on a long gold rod. The mixed-gray-haired banker-looking husband sat at the table. It gave the room an office-looking effect.

He asked me where I came from, how much experience I had had, and after reading my reference he looked me all over and asked me what else I had in mind besides being his chauffeur, and why did I quit John Ringling. I told him I wanted to learn how to sing. He said, "That will be all," and told the maid to call the next man.

I wasn't the lucky bird to get his letter the next morning. I hunted all summer for a job, until election time. Then I got a job with a colored politician, boosting for Whitman of New York City. I was head of the distribution of circulars in Harlem. I had the privilege of seeing and helping to cover every flat in the district. Then I covered Hell's Kitchen and the East Side myself, around 113th Street., where a few colored people live. That job turned out to be a starvation job. The political boss that was to get the money said the Republicans wouldn't pay him off, although Whitman won by a landslide. He gave me six dollars that he said he took out of his own pocket. I worked two weeks for him.

The next week, after election, I got a job at a billiard parlor at 181st Street and Broadway as porter and rack man. That was a fair job but I had to be up there from 11 A. M. until twelve at night. I started to learn the piano in the mornings at home, the only time I had to practise. But a young lady that was working as chorus girl in Ziegfeld's Follies lived there and she complained. (She was colored, but she looked like white.) I held the billiard-parlor job until late November. The business was just getting good when the fellow that had the job the last winter came back. We split the work for a while. Finally, we got into a row over the morning work, and the boss canned me. That was one time I wanted to commit murder. Winter was coming on and me with no job. I had almost starved to death during the summer, after the New Yorkers got through robbing me. I put a couple of more ads in the papers, but no answers came, so I wrote John Ringling that I wanted some kind of a job.

The next week I got a letter from him to come and see him. I went down to the Fifth Avenue apartment, and he had me come in the library. He put me through the third degree about where I had been and what I had been doing and who I had been living with. He didn't find anything wrong with me, so he hired me to take my old job back. We didn't discuss salary. In two weeks' time Mr. Ringling, C. C. Wilson (Ringling's business associate) a Japanese chef and I were rolling over the Erie for Chicago.

In Chicago Ringling told me to press his blue suit with the pin-red stripe in it, as he left the car. In pressing it, I found a twenty dollar bill folded up tight in the left-hand pants pocket. I laughed aloud. The Jap asked me, what I was laughing about. I said nothing. I didn't let him know I had found the twenty dollars. If the bill had not of been folded I might have kept it, as broke as I was, because I would have thought it had slipped off of his big roll like he always carried.

In all the years I had known him I had never known him to fold a bill for anything. He can skin a bill of any denomination out of a roll of money and never ruffle it up. I knew he had set a trap to catch me stealing, if my contact with New Yorkers had so framed my mind to do. The next night the private car was hooked up next to the baggage car on the Chicago, Milwaukee Limited, Montana bound. When C. C. and J. R. came on the car, I waited until the train was pulling out of the station before I gave him the twenty. My, what an expression and pleasing smile came over his face!

We only stayed in Montana ten days, and most of the ten days I spent visiting friends and my people. My mother tried to persuade me to stay home, but I knew I could never stand White Sulphur Springs any more until it gets to be a big city. My old friend of the hills, C. H., was peeved at me because I had worked for the Whitman campaign. He's a good Democrat, and thought he had made me one. But he forgive me when I told him I didn't put any money into the campaign, and I woulda worked as hard for the Democrats, as broke as I was. Also, I didn't expect anything from either party until I could put money into the box to put them in power. The Jap quit in White Sulphur and I had the whole car to man again by myself.

The first breakfast I cooked for J. R. was his old favorite dish. That was one dish I made taste like no other cook he ever had could do, he said. Sautéd Kidneys on Toast. He was hard to cook for. I had to study like the dickens to get the old routine of putting foods together to suit him. J. R. can cook a wicked Spanish omelet himself. He can make an egg stand up like foam on a fresh pail of milk. He told me that when he and his brothers were working in the show, he used to fix SWELL dishes, as he called them.

We went from Montana to Oklahoma. Jake Hammond, the man that got killed by his wife later in Ardmore (and she tried to go in the movies on the strength of it) was Ringling's business partner on oil deals. (That guy Hammond was a wizard with the women!) He had wired Ringling of a big gusher in a new field. Going to Oklahoma over the Rock Island, we had a terrible time with the electrical machine on the car. We lost three belts off the motor put on by different railroad men on the trip. When we pulled into Ardmore, Oklahoma, we were beltless. Ringling told me that he would dine out for a day and for me to put a belt on. I got a new belt from a hardware shop in Ardmore and proceeded to put it on. While I was under the car working on the thing, a swell brown came by. I had been introduced to her before. She was a school teacher. She was surprised to know that I could do something else but cook, and suggested that I quit Ringling and stay in Ardmore. Ringling remained in Ardmore nearly three weeks that trip, and I called on that girl all the time. I had begun to get that giddy feeling again. It was a good thing we couldn't agree on where was the best place to live, or I might have broken my vow to myself about marriage. Thanks to the disagreement, I left Ardmore without buying the ring, but with a good impression in my head that I am born to have tough luck with the ladies.

We came back to Chicago. Mr. Wilson lived there. Mr. Ringling went to New York, and I went with the car to Baraboo, Wisconsin, to take old Al Ringling and his family to Sarasota, Florida. They had a house in the city of Sarasota, not far from the bay. Old Al was failing fast. He couldn't eat anything but special foods—clam broth and milk toast, a little breast of chicken and a little fish, some vegetables. I would set the table with swell dishes and big steaks for the rest of the family and nurse. He'd sit and watch them eat and tell me that he used to be able to eat like that, too. The look on his face had me guessing whether to laugh or cry. He told me I was so good to him he'd give me a fine present, and when he was well, we'd go out to Montana and hunt and fish. But poor old Al died and I never did get anything from him.

John and Mabel soon came to Florida by train for their rest and play. Robert Ringling (we called him Bob), Charlie Ringling's son, who had fallen when he was a kid and broken his hip or something, was kinda crippled, though fat as a butter ball, and for years had to be pushed about in a wheel chair. At that time, he was much better: he just used a cane. He has a good baritone voice, and he was studying singing with a private teacher in their home.

Florida is something like Montana on the water front. If it's a clear night, you could hear Bob singing for ten blocks. He said he'd help me with my music sometime, but that time never came. His father asked me one day why I didn't study. I told him I didn't have enough money and my job travelled too much. He changed the conversation. Bob is singing in concerts, and so am I, and I'll sing in opera, too, if I ever get his kinda money. Maybe I will, as broke as I am. You can't tell.

I worked hard by myself on my voice, as much as I

could. I used to take good records and turn them down slow so that a tenor sounded like a bass and a soprano sounded like a contralto, and steal from them. When the Florida season was over and we came back in New York for the big show, I also sat under great singers there and stole their stuff. Between the two, I was getting along fine.

After the New York run, we were making ready to go west. Mrs. Ringling, who, by the way, was a very charming looking lady, about five feet eight, weighing around 140 pounds, with jet black hair and dark brown eyes, which were very snappy, didn't have any kids. Her dressmaker had just finished her new summer wardrobe. Among the dresses, she had one phantom red all over, shoes to match. He and her was going to the Waldorf-Astoria for late dinner and dance. It was about nine-thirty. I was going by the hall to his room when we all three kinda met. He spied her red dress, her flaming red dress, and made her take it off. I didn't say a thing, but she looked at me. I must have registered the wrong smile, because the next morning she asked me to press the canvas cover that they put over the carpet when they went away for the summer. The canvas is fully twenty feet by forty feet. I told her, yes I'd do it, but the more I thought of it, the more I thought I'd spoiled my job there by knowing too many things.

Then I thought of Ed and Jessie, who had worked for years for Otto Ringling before he died, (and he left millions), yet they didn't get the first dime. I hadn't drawed my full salary since I had started to work for John the second time, until I came to New York on that trip. And because I didn't talk salary to him before I started, I found myself $260 short of what I expected to have, and I couldn't get a big loan from him. All this stuff ran through my head. I said, what's the use of working for a rich man if you can't get help from him. So I quit Ringling again.

CHAPTER 14

POWER IN SHADES

I GOT a job running an elevator in John Wanamaker's store on Tenth Street. Someone told me Wanamaker's would teach anyone music who wanted to learn while they worked there. But when they got through running me up and down in an elevator, there was little music left in me. Once a customer reported me. He told me to open up my mouth when I called off the floors. I told him to take the wax out of his ears. Of course, you know he was spending the money, so naturally he got the verdict from the office. A short time after that, I quit Wanamaker's all fagged out.

I was living with my old friend, Sol Johnson, in Harlem. He got me a position with Uncle Sam to take a crazy man home to the West Indies. It was very interesting work, even if I did have to sleep with him. We went down steerage and I came back first class. We sailed on the older steamer *Priema*. She left New York City two days after the German submarine sank half a dozen boats off the coast of Rhode Island. We just missed her.

On the trip going, the captain and a gang of fellows played poker every day until we hit a hurricane. It was a good thing the boat was loaded down with Ford cars so that she lay close to the water, or we might have sunk. The storm ripped half of the captain's bridge away, killed two mules, flooded the stateroom and just wrecked the kitchen. They had a crazy woman on board, too. The seas were hitting the hardest on her side of the boat. She screamed continually. Somehow, she got out of her cell, and it took six of us big husky men to catch her. Before we could get her into the straight-jacket, she was stripped nude, all but her stockings, and as slippery as a greased pole. My patient was as quiet as a mouse all through the storm. There was a wounded soldier on board, from the battle of the Marne. He died, and a woman committed suicide. I went up into the main saloon, where there were about twenty-five or thirty men and women, black and white, on their knees in six inches of slushing water, singing, *Nearer My God to Thee.* A negro Baptist preacher read a Psalm from a pocket Bible in a near monotone, then read a prayer for God to have mercy. In fifteen minutes' time, the captain stuck his head into the hatchway and hollered down, "The instruments show signs of abatement." Then the mob in there did kick up some fuss.

I learned a great deal about white people and niggers that morning. There were first class white passengers hugging steerage blacks who had been drowned out from below, and I can't say which lot put up the biggest religious fuss. Mother in her palmy days was a novice compared with them.

We were within fifty miles of St. Thomas when the storm started, and a hundred and fifty miles from there the next morning. In St. Thomas, the storm did $2,000,-000 worth of damage. It twisted the large ship's coaling crane up like you'd bend a match stick. We didn't get anything to eat but fruit until we left St. Lucia. Then the sea grew as calm as a lake, and the captain returned to his poker with his friends.

The next morning, I was awakened by a thousand voices shouting like wild men, and as I looked out of the porthole, I saw the boat was surrounded by hundreds of rowboats, each manned by one or two men, soliciting passengers and baggage to take ashore in their water taxis. In less than an hour, I was dressed and passed O.K. by the Port physician, and taken ashore with my crazy man.

In Barbados, they locked me up, and the crazy man, too. Although I had papers to show that Uncle Sam had found Herbert Berkeley insane, the British government didn't believe me nor Uncle Sam. They made me prove it in court and pay two pounds ten for the trial. Can you imagine me, how I felt, face to face with the fellow and trying to tell the judge why he was crazy? He happened to have one of his fits before the court, and I won the case. I took him out to the insane asylum for safe keeping until the ship left for St. Vincent's, his home, a week later. During that week I saw all the interesting places in Barbados—Sam Hill's castle, the penitentiary and the Botanic Gardens.

I was in the theatre the night they first showed the *Battle of the Marne*, a real movie of that great fight. The governors of the island and all the great bosses were there. They sat up on a little Nigger Heaven in the back of the small house. Those seats were considered the best.

I was down front in the pit. Just before they showed the picture, the little orchestra began playing the British National Anthem. Everybody began to sing. I thought it was the same song we used to sing in school, *My Country 'Tis of Thee*. I began singing with 'em—*My Country 'Tis of Thee*. That's as far as I got. Two Englishmen gave me the bum's rush for three aisles, until I heard them linger on *King*. I grabbed that word away up on B flat or high C, I don't know which. At any rate, it sounded that I meant it, and they let me go back to my seat. All through the show I felt uneasy. People seemed to be watching me more than they were the movie.

After the show, natives outside in the street said that I was a West Indian that had been to America and had got a pair of shoes and now I wanted to disown my country. I had met a detective at the court house. He was at the show. After the show he took me around the town to show me some of the inside sights. It was with him that I learned class by color. In the U. S. A., a Nigger was a Nigger, as long as he had one drop of black blood. It's nothing to see a dark girl with a light fellow here, or a dark fellow with a light girl. But in the West Indies, they went according to shades. No white-looking spade would think of going with a real dark one, and all the servants must be darker than the employer. The first party I went to was of the dark mahogany shade. They were all dressed in white clothes. Some were dolled up in a few bright colors, and all the men carried canes. I attended a couple of light parties, by being employed by Uncle Sam. My stocks were sent up and I was passed.

One day I saw a wedding, and everybody was darker than coal but the preacher. That made many things run through my head.

After seeing poverty like I seen in Georgia, I liked the West Indies the best of the two places. At the close of a fast week, the out-bound steamer had me and my patient on board, bound for St. Vincent's, Berkeley's home. It is a beautiful little volcanic island a day's sail from Barbados. We landed there at ten o'clock in the morning. All the populace were down to meet the incoming steamer. The steamer can't go up to the pier there, like they can in some of the other islands. The passengers landed from lighters.

Herbert's father was there to meet him at the pier. After I cleared the customs, we walked slowly up through the narrow, hot streets, into the marvellous Botanic Gardens. Mr. Berkeley wanted to see if Herbert could realize he was at home, and recognize where he used to play. He gazed on them like a child in a toy shop just before Christmas. On up the hill we went. A little creek flowed fast to the sea beside the dirt road, making our gait seem much faster than we were really going. We stopped for breath. The patient's father asked his son many questions, trying hard to make him know his home and friends who loved him. Poor Herbert gazed about like a man drunk from a dazing blow on the head. He never spoke, just nodding his head in answering—sometimes he nodded his head "yes," when the answer should have been "no."

When we got within thirty yards of the house, setting

on the side of a hill that was covered by tropical trees, his old mother came running down the hill, dressed in a knee-length brown dress, no hat or shoes on. Her arms were stretched out to her first born son, who had gone out into the world to get rich, that they might live better—into the world where he lost his mind. I have never seen a more pathetic sight or heard such a heart-rendering conversation in all my life than that morning on the narrow road, when Herbert Berkeley came home to his mother.

Herbert had saved up a hundred and twenty pounds before he lost his mind. This money was in the Boston Dime Savings Bank. I gave the bank book to his father and told him he would have to collect the money through a lawyer. He took the book to an island solicitor from England, a man about fifty years old with white hair, who wore a loose-fitting black Palm Beach suit on his bulky frame, always with a white bow tie, and carried a big baggy hand umbrella, which he used more for a cane. He wanted Mr. Berkeley to pay him forty pounds to collect the money, but Mr. Berkeley come to me at the Hotel with tears streaming down his cheeks like a spanked child might have. He told me his trouble. I knew this fellow was robbing them so I took the bank book.

That evening, I went to the British Home Office, after I had drafted a letter that took me a hour and a half of hard trying in the dictionary to get spelled half right the words I used. To my surprise, he accepted it. He put enough red ribbon and seals on it, that any ordinary person would have thought it was a string of rare pearls to the Queen herself, the way it was wrapped. I never felt happier in my life. I had written a letter the King had accepted and I had a receipt for it. But for doing it, the next morning before I could get out of the shower bath in the yard of the Criethon Hotel, this old duffer was there to see me, sitting in the office talking to Mr. Criethon, the hotel manager.

Mr. Criethon was a light West Indian, who classed himself as white. After I dressed I was called by the little page girl to the office. Criethon introduced me to the solicitor and we all sat down to what I thought was a little chat, but before we had gotten far this old gentleman began to rag me about my position. How did I come to get it? He had heard that no black person in the states had a position higher than a porter. He asked me where I had been and if they still burned my kind in Mississippi: he said he could well understand the reason why. I had a terrible time being a gentleman, he ragged me in such nice English. I was handicapped. I didn't want to let him know my real speed by cussing, especially in Criethon Hotel, and cussing words were my best way of expressing myself, verbs and adjectives. Well, right out of a clear sky phrases came to me that got Criethon to laughing. That upset the old Kodger and he turned on Criethon. I ordered cold beer and cigars while they had it. That was one time I got quick service while I was at the Hotel. The old fellow was so wrought up, the cold black beer hit the spot that needed to be cooled off. He decided that I was too clever for an American negro. I must be a native of the West Indies and we shook hands. He said he wouldn't have me locked up for doing a solicitor's work without a licence, as he came to inform me he was going to do. He bid me Good Morning and said he would see me again.

The day I landed, I met a young fellow who played the violin fairly well . . . we became good friends. He took me all over the Islands. Every morning we used to go swimming. He had a bunch of girls that swam nude with him, also a tribe of Indians he hung out with —I can't remember that tribe's name. We all went out behind a reef of rocks from the view of the city to swim.

One day a gal said to me "Come, lets swim over to that island," pointing across the channel: it looked to me like about a quarter of a mile. "All right," I said. She took out. I was right behind her. She could swim like a water spaniel; I wasn't paying much attention to where she was going—just following her. Finally I looked up. I saw that the island was nearly as far from me as when we started: I knew I couldn't make it. I floated, tread, and did every thing else I knew to keep on top of the water. As I struggled toward the shore I ran my head into a white cap with a black band on it. I treaded again and read the band. It read *S. M. S. Karlsruhe*. I said to myself, a dead man's cap, I guess I'll go to meet him soon; but the girl swam rings around me and kidded me so, I made shore with my tongue hanging out a foot. When I got my breath I examined the cap thoroughly. It belonged to some man named Wisser.

One of the greatest vacations I ever had was a month on St. Vincent's, waiting for the Royal Mail steamer, on which I had booked passage for New York. It arrived one beautiful sunny morning around ten o'clock, and it was five o'clock in the evening when the cargo was taken off and the boat was ready to receive its out-going passengers.

An interesting thing happened when we were leaving the island. Some man was shipping a blood horse to Barbados, and they brought him out to the steamer in a lighter. It was a sad thing that that ship didn't have a place for a horse on it. While they were unloading some of the other things from the lighter, the horse jumped overboard, and started swimming out to sea. They put life saving boats out to catch him. He swam all around the boat for at least an hour, sometimes headed towards shore. He could see the city lights, but he wouldn't go ashore. After a long chase, they caught him and put straps under him to lift him into the lighter. Somehow the straps slipped and caught around his neck, and he was hung. Everyone on board was very sad. He had put up such a gallant swim.

CHAPTER 15

HARD LUCK IN NEW YORK

THE trip to New York was perfectly grand. The sea all the way was beautiful and calm, but when I got into port I found my luck was running hard. Uncle Sam had passed a new law that any steamship company that brought an alien to the U. S. and they went insane, the steamship company that brought him would have to take him back at their own expense. That put an end to that kind of a job for me.

I walked all over New York, put ads in the paper, but I couldn't get a job doing anything in my line. So I shipped with a bunch of men to Connecticut to work in a brass mill. One night of that was enough for me. I almost lost my right hand by a bolt of sharp edged brass. I returned to New York and looked again for work, but it was two weeks before I heard of men being wanted to help finish building Camp Upton. Out there, I was employed as a bricklayer's helper. I saved up over two hundred dollars quickly, in less time than six weeks. They had crap games every night, and I was lucky in them. I came back to New York City for another run of hard luck. Finally, I got a job as Six-man in the dining-car service of a New York railroad. Six-man is the extra man on the Diner; he calls the meals and helps the

waiters, also he waits on people upstairs, as they call the coaches.

My first trip out taught me if I didn't get a line of my own I wouldn't make much money on that job. So I got the chef to put me up a special dish I could drum up upstairs. I was feeding so many of the people upstairs the rest of the waiters kicked. They limited me to ten dinners and all the drinks I wanted to sell. Then I switched my drumming to selling liquor and cut the food, unless someone ordered it for the order. They didn't bother me anymore—a lucky break for me. I got so I could earn from fifteen to fifty dollars a trip up on Seventeen and back on Six, the following morning. Everyone had money and they didn't care who took it.

One night Seventeen was loaded tight, not another vacant space on her. As a rule, on a train that was loaded so heavy, they needed two crews, but our crew could handle it alone—the fastest crew that was ever known to ride that railroad, and a bigger bunch of cut-throats never lived together. Diner 441 was under steward Breakleg, a little red-headed Englishman. The crew was of all colors. Chapman—almost high-yellow, the master mind and pantryman on station 2; Bob Lowe—a high-brown and crafty executor on station 1; William Stewert of Mt. Vernon—a brown and pious exponent of change, station 3; Dickty Jones—a dark brown and real confidence man on station 6; Clayton—a little black boy, that could make a bottle of milk stand on the edge of a glass on a tray when Seventeen was making the bend at Poughkeepsie doing sixty miles an hour, the

Harlequien of the car on station 5; H. M. Oldham—a
brindle, and the Beau Brummell of the car, on station 4.
Small was chef, and he also had the fastest second cook
and dishwasher on the line. The crew was too hot, thats
all, too tight. No signifying with that gang, they laid it.

Well, this night I was talking about, the car up next
to the chair car (next to the baggage coach) had four
men playing poker in stateroom A, with money on the
table—plenty of bills, all sizes from a hundred down—
when I made the call for dinner. It was a hot June evening and Seventeen was shaking her tail around the
bend at Spikendyver.

One fellow said, "Aay—we want som'um to eat here."
I always carried a menu with me, I learned that much
on the western road. After they made their order, another fellow said, "Yes, and we want something to drink,
bring plenty of cold beer. Fill the water cooler up there,"
he said, pointing at the water tank in the wash room.
Just as I was leaving the stateroom, another guy said,
"Hay, ain't you got any women on here?"

"Do you want some?" I said, kind of jesting.

"Sure, bring 'em along," he said.

"Yes, but they cost money you know," I said.

"Oh Hell, bring 'em along," he said.

On my way back to the diner I spied two women sitting in a section in the next car to the diner. One was a
short stout lady, dressed in a blue crepe de chine fine
weave summer dress, too thin to be really a lady. You
could see just how kind nature had been to her. The

other was a little more modest, but she had all the ear-marks of being a regular fellow.

I passed by, put in my order for food, and loaded the drinks on my tray. I made two claret lemonades: I set them on the edge of my tray and started for upstairs. When I got to the ladies, I said in my best tone of voice, "Pardon me, but some gentlemen from New York wants you to have some refreshments with them. I think one is Mr. Ziegfeld." They looked at each other, then at the drink, and reached for it. I lifted it out of their reach. "Not here—up in their car," I said, then stepped off in the lead. I kept telling them, just the next car, for eight pullmans. They almost quit me at the last car. The stout one got leg weary. I always let them see the cool drink when they acted as if they were going back. That helped me a great deal; as hot as it was, they'da walked a mile to get that cool refreshing looking claret.

When they entered the stateroom, the men let out a surprising "Ahaaah," and stood up. The girls were be-wildered to see no one there they knew, but they stayed. I served the party quick, left for the food, served that and added forty dollars—twenty dollars apiece for the women, and the fellow that asked for them paid it with a smile. I almost spat out my heart to think I got the money without an argument.

I don't know how long the girls stayed with that gang, but just before we ran into Utica, where they cut off the diner, these two girls came back into the diner with a man around fifty, who was all drunked up. Dickty Jones set them at Station Six, and they had a few drinks. When the gentleman tried to pay his check he found his wallet gone. The conductor turned the train upside down, he searched every waiter and delayed the train nearly an hour. The next day the laundryman found the empty wallet in the laundry box. How these girls got away with the money, none of us have been able to find out until this day, the way they were dressed.

(Houdini would turn over in his grave if he heard of that stunt.)

In New York City the waiters struck at Churchill's restaurant on Broadway. The management sent word to Harlem that any railroad waiter could get on. That sounded good to me, and I said to myself at last I'll get a chance to make some real bucks. So I left the railroad, and got on. Everything was going fine for me—earning from fifteen to twenty dollars a night. The country was still wet, but we were not allowed to sell liquor to soldiers. A lot of officers were in town. They came into Churchill's nightly. I had a set of tables way in the back. That group and their gals all flocked back there. Somehow they always got plenty to drink: their tables were always loaded down with teapots. So many of them came in and asked for me, the manager thought I was freakish. I was doin' what might be called a land-office business, when the jinks hit me again: some spade didn't pay his check at all, which was for over a hundred dollars' worth of food and we all got kicked out.

I was without a job for a couple of weeks. I had saved up some money, and Will Marion Cook wanted to put on a sketch he said was going to work in a Shubert show called *Levee Days*. He said that if I'd go in and help finance the sketch I'd have a acting part in it, as well as plenty of money. They were rehearsing over in the Lafayette Building on 131st Street. For three weeks I kept the company of men and women, while they whipped things into shape. We went over to Gibson's Theatre in Philadelphia to break the sketch in. Everything was going down fine and it looked like a sure hit, but when Saturday night came all the money for the sketch had been drawn in advance to pay for a wardrobe for the New York opening. So we had to work for Gibson the second week, to be able to pay off the room rent and board bills for the company in Philly.

At the close of the second week we just had enough money left to get to New York.

In New York I quit the show business after it had almost broke me. I took my last sixty dollars and had some special woman's underwear and nightgowns and shimmies of silk and crepe-de-chine, designed by myself, made on Allen Street, New York. I peddled that stuff from door to door in Harlem until I joined the army.

At that time, they were talking so much of peace that I had a hunch I wouldn't get killed. I was too lucky in the draft. I registered from Ringling's residence, and, being black in a white neighborhood, they couldn't place me until the war was nearly over. I knew I would have been crazy to join the army with a free will. At one time of my life, I would have been glad to join the army voluntarily, but after I found out Uncle Sam's money was half bogus to me, and things weren't just the same as they were when we kids used to drill during the Spanish-American war days, I had changed my mind, although I didn't claim any exemption.

When Uncle Sam sent me the Greetings to join his army, he said in his letter, "Bring no jewelry." During the time I was railroading, I had found a diamond bracelet in a lady's purse in 42nd Street, as I came out of the Grand Central one day. It had over seventy-four diamonds in it. I looked in all the papers for a lost ad. None were to be found, so I kept it. Obeying Uncle Sam's orders, I put the bracelet in pawn at Simpson's on Broadway for one hundred and seventy-five dollars. I didn't want to put it in heavy because I thought if I ever came out of the war I would get it out. But when I came out of the army camp, in some way I never could figure out, detectives gyped me out of it. I never did see the owner, and I bet she never got the bracelet.

I only stayed in the army six days. They turned me out one of the highest paid men in the army . . . eleven dollars a day and some cents.

It was in Camp Dix in Jersey that I had a chance to sing for over two thousand hard-boiled rookies. They gave me a big hand and I was convinced that if I could make that gang like me I would be a hit in an audience of men and women together. When I returned to New York City, Rosamund Johnson was leaving the settlement school with an act for vaudeville.

I had studied some music with Johnson at the school during my spare time when railroading. The first time I sang publicly with him playing the piano was for a week at Wanamaker's Auditorium, during a Lincoln's Birthday celebration. The next time was on a benefit bill in the Hammerstein Opera House during the war. The bill was full of big artists. I was scared pink. I had to sing after Mme. Alda and she had stopped the show. It was a good thing I was singing Harry Burleigh's war song, *When The Boys Come Home*, or I might have been swamped.

The third time took the prize. Reverend Brown had just sold his flat church on 137th Street. He and his flock had bought the big sandstone church on 128th Street and Seventh Avenue. He had planned a big Rally Sunday, and he wanted a special attraction, so he got J. Rosamund Johnson and Mr. Johnson got me. He told me we would be paid according to the amount of money they raised—ten percent on the dollar. We went down to the church and sat in the back row, near the 128th Street entrance. Brown lived across the street. The church was jammed. After we had waited a half hour, Brown's brother or son (I don't know just what his position is in the family) with another fellow, walked in the door and down the aisle side by side, up into the pulpit. The solemn congregation sat as still as mice, and the day was hot. The brother opened the services by telling about what was going to happen the following week. He made a short prayer and sat down. No sooner than he sat down than Brown came into the church, dressed in a long black robe, flowing from his six-foot shoulders. The congregation all stood. When he got into the pulpit, he waved them to be seated. Then he begin telling them what he

167

wanted. He said he had arranged to have a special musical for them, but they couldn't hear it until they all came up and laid nothing less than a dollar on the table before him—that the church must be paid for quick. The mob of over a thousand people poured up to the table and laid their money down. Some dropped five dollar bills. My mouth began to water, as hungry as I was, I could see ham and eggs and chicken and lamb all cooked well before me. I had been stuck up with a gun the week before and my rations were kinda short. Mr. Johnson played the organ and I sang *If With All Your Hearts You Truly Seek Him, Ye Shall Surely Find Him.* But it wasn't so with that money. I have never gotten a dime to this day.

I had sung in the Salem church choir for two reasons while I was selling silk underwear. It was a fine chance to study music, and I had a good bunch of customers among the chorus. But I quit all church work after that, and I joined Johnson's act. For three years we travelled the B. F. Keith circuit from coast to coast, south as far as St. Louis, north to Moose Jaw, Canada. The first date we played was in Jersey City. I played the banjo in the jazz band and sang a love song. The vaudeville crowds got my goat, and my knees began to shake. I had a pair of white flannel trousers on, and to keep the audience from seeing my knees trembling, I began to walk up and down the stage. But the song was the hit of the act. Sometime later, the tenor singer in the quartet, quit. I took his place, and they got another drummer. The fellow that quit used to play the drums, too.

My vaudeville travels put me in contact with lots of noted singers that helped me on the fine points in the game. Then Johnson decided that he wanted a bass fiddle in the act. My brother Bob happened to have one at home. I sent for it, and learned to play it, but it cost me so much money to keep it fixed that I really didn't get much out of vaudeville. One time coming from Canada, they broke my bass fiddle case open to see if it had whiskey in it. When I opened the box in St. Paul, my fiddle looked like an orange crate.

Our violinist quit in Minneapolis. His grandmother died, and we picked up another young fellow there. His name was Leon. Then we went to Milwaukee, where he fell in love with a young girl. They corresponded all the way to the coast and back. In Kansas City, I got mixed up with a married woman who liked the song I was singing. When we hit Chicago, both women were there. We all four went out cabareting. It was about four A. M. when I told my buddy to take his young lady home and not kiss her good-night. He said, "Aw, you and Pete are old and fogey."

"Go ahead. You'll see," I said. I gave him the same protection that Tom Owens had given me in St. Paul when Mrs. Scott had wanted me to meet a church girl. I could look at Leon's Milwaukee girl, and tell she would be like a new-born meadow in a spring rain if you just threw a kiss at her. Well, about three weeks later, there came a telegram to him saying, "Honey, I miss you so much. Do come back soon." A few days later we went down to the theatre one morning for rehearsal at eleven

A.M. There was a second telegram there for him. It read: "Baby, My head aches, and my left breast is sore."

I didn't want to say nothing to Leon, but I knew it wasn't the last news he'd get from that baby. Sure enough, the very next day came a third, saying, "What am I going to do? Find me a doctor."

I knew a doctor, a friend of mine, in Chicago. We took a night run up to see him, to see if he'd take the case. He asked how old was the girl. When we told him seventeen, he threw up his hands and shook his head. Then we found a fellow that would take the case, but she would have to go blindfolded to his office and leave the same way. She wouldn't consent to that kind of treatment, so my buddy married her.

* * *

I was working on an invention at the time for a plier collar to wear on the stage, to cut the laundry bill. I had paid the first fee to the patent attorney, when some young lady gave Johnson the idea for what they thought was the song of the century, named *June*. He insisted upon me singing it in place of *The Girl You Love*, which I was stopping show after show with. During rehearsal, we tried to show him it was a dog. But you know how people are with their own children. I was to sing it, with a dreadful obligato to it sung by one of the men in the company. I gave it two good fair chances with liberal audiences. It fell flat. That convinced me he should put it with the paper in the rolls. I told chief not to play that song for me any more or I'd walk off the stage if he did. That meant quit for sure. It was not only insulting him, but the audience as well. That night, in a packed house in an upstate theatre, when I walked on with the drums (I brought them on to camouflage the audience) he started the vamp of *June, The Night Is Sighing.* I felt a cold chill run down my back. Never would I let that beautiful audience set tight on me. I left the stage. The rest of the company tried to sing the song. It was arranged too high for any of them and too low to sing the octave under it. So they tried to transpose it at sight. My Gawd, the result pretty near put everybody in the street. Of course, I left in two weeks.

I didn't bother any more with the invention. I went back to Montana for a rest. During that time, I took my brothers and sister and put on a couple of shows. I made more money than I ever made at one time in my life.

I returned to New York in November and quit singing. I made whiskey for some time, until the lady I was living with wanted too much of my profit. Then I tried laying bricks, but the Union wouldn't let me go there. I had had some experience before, but I didn't have a card. When I failed at that, I tried working on the docks for a good reason. From that, I played the part of lounge lizzard for men who couldn't find time to take their wives out.

I also worked on an invention I had to pump water on dry land farms. I lost most of my money on that deal. I'll tell the world, having parts made for inventions is the most costly pleasure I know of. One thing I did do: I had the idea of Timkin bearings for railroad cars long before they started, and I tried to get Mr. John Ringling to put them over for me, but he couldn't see it. Then I worked on an idea to make the subways noiseless, but I couldn't find a thing that would stand the friction and heat.

By that time, all my money was gone, and I owed my landlady a terrible rent bill. She had suggested for me to teach Madame Alelia Walker how to drive a car. Somehow or other, I didn't get the amount of money she thought I should have gotten for the job, and she put me out in the street. But Mrs. Walker was my life-saver. She had a big empty house in town, and she gave me a room to stay there as long as I wanted to.

CHAPTER 16

MY PEOPLE

IN all and all, I convinced myself that my people were as hard to figure out as perpetual motion. I have never been able to find out why they pull apart so much. With all the opportunities they have had since the Civil War, if they were a noble people, there is no way to convince me they would stay in the South under the most trying conditions and leave the millions of acres of unsettled land west of the Mississippi lie dormant. Being that the white man classes all niggahs alike, though he treats 'em different, the mystery to me is why they don't join together as one big tribe. I have white people tell me they will soon, but I don't think this generation will witness it, unless the white people have it up their sleeves that they are soon going to send all negroes back to Africa or some-other place.

To me the white and colored people are like a man and wife—can fight all they please with each other, but let some one else step in and they both will hop on them, Teeth and Claws. Maybe it's the different mixture of white blood in them; there's hardly a negro left in the U. S. A. that has a pure stream of black blood left in his veins. Is it possible that we could get more of an analysis of the negro if only one caucasian race had lost control of their loins? It is too bad that such a despised race can be impregnated by others than their own. But who knows? Maybe niggahs and dogs are closely related. When I used to breed dogs out west, I found that if a female dog was first mated with a blooded dog, it made no difference who the father of the second litter of pups was—there was always a pup or two with the ear-marks of the first mate. If that's so with the negro, some day we might get a group of them that will trust and act like great business men.

I will admit this would be a terrible world to live in if we didn't have the niggahs and latins to mix their play—rhyme and music with life.

When the white strain of blood shows itself a little more, probably the Negroes won't accept anything like Christianity. The main reason for accepting it now is because they think they are getting something for nothing. Every Negro should know why there are not large perpetual motion machines that could fly from here to Europe and back without stopping, or from here to Mars: if they did, they wouldn't be so pious. They would realize that if there is a God he is a scientific God. You can't get something for nothing, that will stand up.

Illiterate white people are more annoying to me than ignorant blacks for this reason: the blacks do seem to enjoy their three major activities—working, playing and participating in the strong desire nature put in animals to perpetuate their living on this earth. After all, they seem to have combined the motive powers of life. Whites may enjoy these achievements, too, but if they do I wonder why they are so silent about them. Sing loud doing your duties if you like them.

I think the churches would be a grand thing for my people if they used them right. If they learned their lesson good from the white people who taught them religion, they would know it could be used for a thrifty purpose as well as a divine one. Whenever the white religious teachers want any land or precious goods, the big heads of the God-fearing business get together and send a small band of missionaries out where the desired material is, to tell the heathen natives about the Great Judge on High who will give them everything they can imagine they would like to have when they die, if they will bring the fat of their land to the missionaries as long as they have strength to carry it. There has been little grumble from the gracious heads of the heavenly solicitors because of the puny payments the ungrateful pagans are giving for their admission to the land of living peace.

Although the essence of the instructions for the missioners seems almost fool-proof, on close investigation you might find a very important subject left out. Of course you can't censure the Great Chancelors for overlooking the topic, because looking at it would cause them embarrassment, so *they left it out*. They didn't say, "My dear missioners, be sure to keep this steel-studded belt about your loins. It is well made and you can wear it in your bath as well as sleep in it. If you once grow weary of guarding it, some lustful heathen maid might steal some of the sacred seeds of our pious and noble plant, and could sow them in their filthy weedy gardens. Then

—who knows—some of their wise men could graft our precious flower to some prickly plant and the union will produce a peculiar kind of thistle. . . . Surely, missioners, you know what a thistle will do near a cultured meadow in seeding time: if the wind happens to be blowing the right way?"

(Perhaps some poor weak missioner slipped the steel girdle off for some reason, because not long ago I was riding in a sleeper and about three A. M. a man high up shouted, "Thistles! Thistles! Thistles everywhere!" . . . I hope he was dreaming.)

In my travels, I have learned most Negroes are pagans, though they might tell you they are Christians like white people claim to be.

Everything the Negro does has to be censored by the white man before it can be released. And, as a rule, when he sets it free, the average layman thinks it's a white idea. In my school days, I never did read in any of the white histories about free Negroes owning slaves before the Civil War, nor of any Negro book publishers. If there are any, I guess they only print Bibles. But there is one broad-minded caucasian whom I would like to thank, the one who published the books that kept me from committing suicide when I was in love, and believed my people had always been the inferior race, a band of slaves. That particular infatuation started me reading everything I could get my hands on, and was the cause that lifted high the dark shadows on my life before me, never to return since. I paid many a sleepless night for my admission into the light.

Somehow one of Dr. Hackensack's fine scientific stories fell into my hands about a man who had found how to mix a handful of atoms with an ounce of dust and blow the earth up. For weeks I went to libraries to read books on chemistry thinking I might get an inkling of the ingredients that could destroy this old earth and everything on it. During those reading hours I found out so far as man is concerned (He) can't destroy anything—glass, paper, or flesh. He may change them into gases or some other material but he cannot destroy anything on this earth. The last day I attended the library on my search, I left convinced I was losing my mind brewing on man's conceived and legislated ideas about life.

I had learned most of them were handed down by egoistic weaklings, especially those I was most interested in (marriage). A priest, Bishop, or Justice of the Peace, can give you the legal right to live together as man and woman, but they cannot give you a guarantee that the couple can continue their living in their offspring. That flaw in the laws caused me to think deeper. I remember our old white she-cat married Higgens's maltese Tom; Jay Anderson's spotted bird-dog succeeded in winning R. G. White's water-spaniel's love; Zentner's short-horned Bull broke down the fence to seduce Sherman's two-year old herfords, and they all had families. Then my mind cased the birds and wild animals of the forests of different species; the fish of the sea, all with no restrictions to make love, yet only those belonging to the same family can reproduce themselves. My thoughts came back to man, and I marked him down as one class, only in different dominating positions, like the fish and animals.

*   *   *

It was one beautiful moonlight Tuesday night that the enchanting woman I had almost lost my mind over and I motored out on the Hudson River Drive. We stopped the car on a high cliff overlooking that majestic stream. After spending a little while carressing each other our conversation led into discussing ways and means to live and be happy. Her family and mine. She had confessed to her father when they put her through the third degree one night when she got home at three A. M. (on account of motor trouble) that a man of another race was her headache. She said her mother cried the rest of the night and her father raved for three days. He threatened to murder her if she left the house again for anything, without her mother. It had been nearly five weeks since I had seen her, and we lived again in conversation every moment spent during our separation. She suggested that we go to South America or Europe, where the people seemed to be higher educated, as she put it. Then came the discussion of livelihood. What could be my vocation? She had been to Europe and knew most all Europeans expected intruding Americans to have loads of money. Three hundred dollars was my bank roll. Her people had money to burn, but there was no chance of my doing a Count stunt, so that was out.

Suddenly, the moon cast the most beautiful glow on the Hudson I have ever seen, although I have been on the same spot many times. We recognized the splendor and beauty but little was said about it. Instead, words in hateful phrases poured forth about the people of our country. I don't believe two people anywhere had thought of more hateful things to say about their native land than we did. We worked ourselfs up to the highest pitch of anarchism, our eyes spitting forth fiery flashes of revenge.

I was never much on praying for some unknown power to help me, but my love had a strong faith in one of the high churches, and she got out of the car, knelt down, using the running-board to rest her elbows on like a pew, and prayed fervently. It was so convincing that I got out and knelt down beside her and begged with all my heart to be helped out of this trying situation. We prayed until large tears were rolling down her cheeks. It seemed that we both had satisfied ourselves and a con-solation would be at hand soon. We raised to our feet together, in unison and silence. A large sparkling star caught our eyes, blinking like a clown in a circus striving to make people laugh. It held us spell-bound for a few seconds, then we gazed at each other and smiled. Then we looked at the grandeur of the Hudson, the thousand little lights on the other side. I told her of the mighty Rockies. This beauty before us, and the imaginary pictures I painted of the West, filled us with happiness. Then we had a good laugh and decided we were silly like little kids to think of exiling ourselves from the beauty nature had put before us, and our native land. We discussed the pros and cons of the sincerity of Omar

Khayyam, when he said it was alright for two lovers to commit suicide. It was a lucky thing that I had read that day where Omar Khayyam had spent a happy youthful life in the cities and later days up in the hills, surrounded by charming women, wine and song. Also he was nearly a hundred years old when he died. So we decided not to depart to the unknown just because years ago a cold-blooded King once made a law to shield his debility and we now felt compelled to accept it, but were prevented because another hypocrite introduced a later law forbidding us from using the first one without being censored. So, we baptised each other in salty tears, and vowed to live according to nature's laws and be happy. That night in bed I thought of everything we had talked about. I felt I was a wicked man. I had dammed people because they were on top. I had hated people of other colors for no personal reason except ignorance on my part. I made a vow to myself I would like all people to play the game of life with nature's rules, then fell to sleep.

The next morning I was awakened by some church workers collecting funds from door to door for some rally. I dropped a coin into the box before I thought of the millions my people give annually to the church, and nothing but a few houses to show for it—most of them mortgaged to the hilt. In Omaha alone, they have this year fifteen churches of one denomination, and no hospital. In New York City, colored people have at least one hundred churches, and not one first-class hotel where you can take a group of business men to a luncheon for a financial proposition.

Colored people throw away enough money to have every facility the White man has if they would join together. They tell me there are twelve million Negroes in the United States. I know a dollar from each person could be put in a treasury monthly to support their own. The Colored people who want to be white so bad, don't seem to realize that while they themselves might pass a certain ethical examination, the negro as a race is a funny animal.

If James Weldon Johnson or Paul Robeson or Dr. DuBois, all three college men, were dining in the Plaza, and a spade dock-hand should spy them there, if he had any money in his pocket, he'd want to go in, too. And he would start a roccous if the manager told him he couldn't dine in there, dressed as he was, let alone his idea of the menu—which he would look all over, and then call for ham and eggs, whether it was on the bill or not.

Dicky colored people do not spend enough time spreading the cultured information they have gained to their neighbors; if they did, maybe those theatre tickets ordered over the telephone might not be cancelled when they show up at the box office for them. I have had two concerts cancelled because dicky niggahs in two towns claimed the concert management was jimcrowing them when he wouldn't give them seats held for years by white patrons. Why should he? These same old patrons had been coming to concerts of all artists for years, no matter what color, while the same dicky niggahs would never attend a concert given by one of their own race, unless they thought they would be in a conspicuous place in a white section. No management can depend upon colored people to hold up their end in art, they will not recognize any negro artist until the white man says he is O. K. . . . Although they have good judgment, you would need a gattling gun to make them be the first to stand back of it.

In the sixteen years I have studied my people, I dislike to belittle my father's judgment. He told mother Zulus were noble people. I don't know how many Zulus were brought to America, but before I mark all spades down in my mind, I will say that in developing themselves as a group, we are no damn good. . . . I must go to Zululand.

Many places where I used to go unmolested, I return to find some uncouth niggah has been there and fixed it so I can't get in again. Even in England, when Florence Mills and her Blackbirds were set free, the niggahs proved their colors as a group. They fought all over the place. Their American manager told the English not to let them eat and dance in their cafés and restaurants, because they couldn't do it at home. Some of the members of that company told me if anyone tried to stop me from going anywhere just say I wasn't a Blackbird, and it would be allright. Yet this American manager lives off negro talents. Would you believe it, there are places right here in beloved Harlem, run by white men, where negroes can't go unless they are jimcrowed? And yet, negro talents are the foundation of the business!

No, sir; there isn't one negro big enough among the two hundred thousand that can put an end to this condition in the heart of their own district.

One of the most amusing things I have heard was at Carnegie Hall on April 16th last. Nathaniel Dett directed the Hampton Institution Chorus. It was the greatest demonstration of how my people hate to be themselves. He had a large group of good voices and they were trained to sing negro spirituals like an Episcopal choir would sing a Greek Easter greeting on that great Sunday morning. Well, there's nothing I can do about this. You might think I intend to run for President . . . but I don't "choose" to. These are my views of my people, so there it is. Now I'll return to the good dirt.

CHAPTER 17

WITH MISS ANN AND MISTER EDDIE

FOR many years I came in contact with lots of cultured people, better known to the American Ethiopian as Miss Ann and Mister Eddie. But in the majority of these positions, I had a queer sort of feeling, as if I was a chair or car or any useful kind of object. When this queer sensation first struck me, all my senses sent messages to my brain at once, which caused a terrible congestion in my mental switchboard. WRATH (the loser of all battles) was dictated to every important control of my body. But when I gained consciousness, I realized that if I wanted to be successful in service, I must radiate the impression that I could only use my senses when they were wanted for someone else's use—like one might press a button or ring a bell or start a machine.

It is impossible for me to explain the Grand and Glorious sensation I get now when these people tell me, by intuition or by spoken word:

"We are tired of that bunk you have been radiating, that you shouldn't use all your senses for yourself!

"You hear that?

"See this!

"Feel his.

"Touch mine.

"Smell her's.

"What does it taste like?"

So don't think I'm full of ego when I relate my experiences with Miss Ann and Mr. Eddie. . . . Just fate, that's all.

* * *

In 1925 J. Rosamund Johnson, who was getting out a book of negro spirituals, asked me to join him, and after the book was published, we set out to sing these songs. Carl Van Vechten, the Abraham Lincoln of negro art, introduced us to Mr. Lawrence Langner, who gave us the Guild Theatre on a Sunday night for our first concert.

I never shall forget the first time I met Carl Van Vechten in his 55th street apartment. We were cordially received and ushered into his sitting room, beautifully decorated with ornaments of rare value setting about the place. Books! One only finds more in Libraries. He was dressed in a long green lounging gown. The soft collar of his white silk shirt was standing wide open and his white hair stood up like a music-master's over his large red forehead. His pure blue eyes have a piercing affect that mighty near stopped my breath for fear: I said to myself, at last I am before Old Pilate himself. If I can pass this examination I will be O. K. and if I can't, never no more singing. He talked very nice as if he wanted to make me feel at home and could see I was nervous, frightened stiff. But those eyes never changed. Thanks to good luck he was not a prohibitionist, and he really knows how to mix a cocktail out of the happy land. His first cocktail would put me out ordinarily, but that day it simply steadied my nerves.

We sang for him and he was pleased. We thought he was all alone in the apartment, but after a few numbers—lo and behold (as the surprise says), a feminine voice from behind the french doors that separated the parlor from the boudoir began setting up a cry of approval. In a few moments, who came out, clad in a Japanese robe, but a bewitching creature five feet six, exquisite figure, dark eyes, fascinating face with a head full of jet black hair and keen feet! She turned out to be the great actress, Carl Van Vechten's wife, Fania Marinoff. She and Mr. Van Vechten passed a few words between themselves, and we were asked to sing again. That afternoon led to all our success.

At that time we had only three spirituals prepared to sing but in three weeks time we gave a concert. The group of new made friends, with the publicity headed by the Lion-Wolf-and-Tiger-hunted little Bunny, Miss Rita Romilly, packed the theatre to the doors. That audiences' approval paved the way for us to sing for the rich, poor, and royalty.

On my trips in concert and entertaining, I have met most of the world's talked-of people, and their actions or words have framed my mind to get lots of enjoyment out of life. You might think poor niggahs in America are altogether handicapped people. I must tell you, there are only three things they don't do without an argument anywhere in the land. Colored people can't eat and sleep where they might want to, even if they

have a pocket full of money. They can't rent a house where their fancy may lead them, or work in all positions they might be qualified to fill. EVERYTHING ELSE UNDER THE SUN THEY DO, all over the country, and most educated people know it. So don't be surprised at anything I might say.

Among the great people I have met, for an American, Heywood Broun is an ace high straight flush. His manners under the most trying social debut has convinced me, since I have seen so many others in an equal position.

Mr. Johnson and I happened to be some of the guests that were invited to the Broun town house on West Eighty-third Street, to meet some Big English Lord and Lady. There never was such a gathering at the League of Nations as there was at Broun's that night— unless they had some Gypsies in the League. Even then, you would need a Heywood Broun to mix the cocktails. There are three people in New York that really know how to mix a cocktail so that a party is sure fire success— Heywood Broun, Carl Van Vechten and Eddie Wassermann. This night, Broun had made a tub full of his favorite drink, and he wasn't keeping it for a party the following week; it was for that night only—all first comers knew it.

The main guests of honor were to come in after some theatre party. All the rest of the supers for the grand sitting were on hand an hour ahead of time, so you know how the cast was feeling, with their thoughts inspired by the ingredients from the tub. The stage setting took up the whole main floor of the Broun mansion. The long parlor, with a big divan that filled up the space in front of the four street windows, was loaded down with an intellectual cast selected from Staten Island to Harlem. The fireplace in the west hall had a real piece of coal burning in it. A grand Ampico piano made a kinda sand-clock effect between the south and north room. In this north room they have a six by six not over a foot high French divan, better known as a Main Bunk, because it was originated in the Main Woods by some Mrs. Smith, a mother of a go-back-to-nature cult. If some one told you how many different conversations can be held on that piece of furniture at once, you'd say a lie. Plenty of soft pillows were chucked in corners, and vacant spots on the floor for those who live close to nature, so that they might feel at home in their sitting position.

The fascinating hypnotic creature, Miss Ruth Hale, was the mistress of ceremonies and stage director. It is uncanny how her conversation did intrigue each actor and actress into the position they best filled, unconscious of their being so placed. All the time during the suspension for the curtain to rise (that was, when the exalted guests were to appear on the scene) Broun was in his shirt sleeves, perfectly all right for a man in his own home or wherever he pays rent. Ten minutes before the grand opening, he laid down on the floor in front of the big divan in the north room. He began discussing some of the early Brouns—paintings of landscapes and city chimneys—with a charming lady.

The door bell rang. The maid and the mistress of ceremonies disappeared into the hall. Semi-silence creeped over the stage. The Big Sticks were ushered into the front room. You have never seen so much bowing and scraping in all your life than was done that night, when Miss Ruth Hale said eloquently with a graceful gesture, "Ladies and gentlemen, Lord and Lady So-and-so," and proceeded to make each individual acquainted with the King's Henchman. I was picked! When I saw Heywood Broun never change his position until sometime after all were made known to each other, I wondered if Broun caught the Lord off his guard in Piccadilly Circus, or Leicester Square, or else, if I traced his pedigree far enough back, I would find a King or Something—or else is he the only emancipated American?

This was one of the first big parties of people famous in the different arts I attended. They have been going on continuously since, and these new friends have opened up a brighter path in life for me.

For instance, Muriel Draper. What a great place this world would be if everyone was free of their inhibitions like Princess Muriel Draper is. Having the greatest wisdom of any and being a marvellous writer, is not enough for her. She knows how to drape her shapely figure in all materials—window curtains, silk bedspreads, satins, Spanish shawls—so that no matter where or how big the party may be people always ask, Who is that woman?

Although Geoffrey Scott has been knowing her for years, she still has got him bewildered. Someone told him I was a bit of a clairvoyant and palmist, so once at a party he asked me what I thought he could do to keep the princess interested. I told him I could see that the woman had twelve magic rings to lock the golden charm deep, that from one to seven of these latches have been sprung, but the fortress fronting the golden hall still remains intact. So the ruffian or Apollo who would scoop shimmering trinklets must find the Amulet that the King of the Centaurs wore, then march gently toward the Princess, who might then bring forth her precious possessions from the golden hall, and decorate him with them. Geoffrey said in beautiful English accents, "Very well; I understand it all. Success shall be mine when I return."

I haven't seen him since.

* * *

You really can not understand what American Tragedies are unless you know many of our country's millionaires who don't know how to play. They should experience Theodore Dreiser's hospitality and know the Crown Prince of Sweden's congenialities. I was pleasantly surprised at the Crown Prince's interest in our singing, particularly Negro Songs. Since I have read *Showboat*, I can understand why Edna Ferber listens so attentively to spirituals, but it will always have me up a tree why a certain critic cries when he hears them sung, when he's glad John Brown is dead.

It was the music-loving Mr. and Mrs. Alfred Knopf

that gave Mr. Johnson and me the privilege of singing for some of the world's greatest conductors and movie celebrities. The Knopfs are the kind of hosts that always give you a thrill in producing new groups. One can never imagine whom you will meet there.

During the last few years I have been around lots of music and I notice that music has a peculiar effect on people. I think this reaction alone has held my interests more than anything else. The higher I go the more interesting I find it. Now, take the piano for instance. I have heard it played all my life: the best I have ever known it to do was to make people sing or dance. I didn't know it could be played to make people cry (like a violin) until I heard Alexandrisco play, and saw a room full of women cry one afternoon at Stanley Spiegelberg's Fifth Avenue apartment. All were sober too. After that I began to watch closer the effect of the spirituals on people. I have grown to really enjoy singing them, even if I do have to concentrate hard on dead people (chiefly my mother) so I can get their interpretation. The dead people I think of sang them in true Christian belief. A spiritual makes some people cry, others laugh, and arouses another's passion. All these things can be done with one song. I don't know any other music that can get the same results. . . . When I sing to people, ten thousand sing to me.

Next came the time for our appearace before senior groups of dowagers, whose guests thrilled me to see. Most of them wear tiaras of diamonds and precious stones. In these groups I usually found that annoying old man who always wanted to upset the host's programme by insisting we sing a hot number he could join in with, that he might vamp the most unsophisticated young girl in the party. If you know society, you know him.

My next exciting experience was when we were engaged to sing by one of the middleaged hostesses who entertain the four hundred. These gigs came through our manager. I loathed the beginning of it—my first one. We arrived at the mansion and the butler had us wait in a little side room, with a pitcher of water on the table and two cigars. Mr. Johnson was happy because black coffee and cigars are his heart. I said to myself what kind of a performance did these people expect from me on water? Not even Canada Dry Gingerale. I thought they would never get ready for us to sing. It was long about eleven o'clock when they finished Dinner and the guests gathered in the music room. We presented our programme. After singing three or four groups of songs we were invited into another room to dinner, and the guests seemed to be leaving. I thought the party was over. But when we were about finished eating, the host came to us and said gleefully, "Well, now all the stiff backs are gone, we'll have some fun. When you are through come into the music room." Mr. Johnson and I took our time with the desert and coffee, thinking we would kill at least two groups.

When we returned to the music room there were about twelve people left of the party. "Ah, here they are. Champaign, champaign, Garcon," the hostess said, and snapped her fingers. In a few moments the butler returned with a rope around his neck tied to a tray loaded down with champaign. We all drank up, then the singing began. The group sang every song hit for the last thirty years. It was nearly four a. m. when I fell in bed asleep at home full of pleasant dreams.

Parties!

*   *   *

I have found the concert business very interesting because of the effect the different audiences have on me when I walk before them. Some give me the most pleasing sensation, others make me feel like stepping into a packing house refrigerator. Of the different songs I sing— some like these and some like those. To watch their faces is amusing. I loathe singing where I can't see an audience and audiences faces. And I also found they are much harder to control in the dark. I have had some peculiar things happen while singing. I wouldn't call myself a natural musician; I have had to study hard the music I have learned. Now, my brother George can go to a show and come back and play the tunes he heard there on the piano, and he had never had a lesson. Another thing, I don't like to hold a sheet of music and sing from it, although I have had to. I usually memorize everything I sing.

A funny thing happened to me in Tuskeegee. Mr. Johnson and I were giving a concert there with Clarence C. White for the school. The auditorium was packed. More than 3,000 people were present. Not many whites in the audience. I had sung the first twelve measures of

Stand Still, Jordan when I heard a jazz band playing. I moved down to the end of the piano and it got louder. Then I moved back, and I could still hear it. I stopped singing, and looked at Mr. Johnson. He was playing *Stand Still, Jordan.* I made him start all over again. That audience couldn't understand what was the matter with me, and I was afraid to tell them: they would of thought I was crazy. But I heard that jazz band playing. I never stood on that spot any more that night. A peculiar radio effect.

From Tuskeegee, we sung our way out west to Los Angeles. We sang for the mighty Behime and Oppenheimer concert circuit in the state of California. Then we went to Portland, and from Oregon into Montana. I had sung many times at home before, but it was the first time I had put on a real concert for my home folks. They showed the most wonderful appreciation. Then we came on back east, making many stops.

CHAPTER 18

MY TRIP TO HEAVEN

AFTER this tour, friends advised us to go to Europe, so we booked our passage and we were to sail in a few days for Europe, better known as Heaven to all American Spades that have been there. I was busy as a bee in July, getting ready for the trip. In all my travels, none took me to Europe before. The tales I heard about it thrilled me, and my pious ofay friends were much perturbed about my going, thinking the experience might make me never want to sing the spirituals again. To get too intimate with the angels would be bad for a worshipper of mythology, they thought. I almost died laughing at times to myself, the things they would say to me, like, You won't be a virgin no longer, for the angels are given free range to live with no inhibitions to govern their descretions in their domain. Somehow they thought I might be a good pupil under these teachings.

The night before I sailed, friends gave many a party to which I was invited. I put my head in to say goodbye to each group. I was like a bird, I jumped from limb to limb all night long. I never realized I knew so many people in New York City that were glad of my chance to see Europe. It was six A. M. when I got home to pack my bag. I learned one thing that night . . . never wait until the day you sail to pack your bag. You really should send it to the boat the day ahead with your trunk.

After the noisy, loving, crying goodbye send-off people gave the departing passengers at the pier, I was sure we were embarked for Heaven. People acted just like they do at big funerals I've attended . . . some crying because the dead one is· gone from this active life . . . others because they love them . . . and some crying for the loss of their whole support. Then there is that character that stands around like the ones at a funeral . . . thinking of the two million dollar will, wondering if their name is on ˉthe list. And there are those with the strange chessy-cat grin, that is hard to interpret just what is going through their minds.

It was one-thirty P. M. May 20th, 1927, when I fell dead asleep in my stateroom on the *S. S. Rochambeau* as she sailed down the harbor. I didn't awake until *dejeuner* was called in the hall outside of my cabin door. In a half stupor I felt my head. It was bursting from the engineering of a stiff job I had piled on it as chief director of the clearing department of the body, so that the storage house might eliminate the conglomeration of food jammed in the night before . . . stuffed olive . . . solami . . . fish . . . steak . . . bad gin . . . good gin . . . pure scotch . . . boiled eggs . . . spinach . . . spanish food . . . cup-wine . . . champagne and misplaced kisses. What a marvellous machine we poor mortals are made of. I certainly was dead.

Dejeuner! *Dejeuner*! What did that mean? My head was so buzzing I couldn't understand that word in the new language. To me it must be something good. I was like a baby. I could make plenty of noise, but no one could understand what I wanted. I had heard that anyone who didn't live right during the week before they sailed, they would have to pay for it on the trip. The passenger next to me must have been very bad, for the punishment he was going through. "Oh, Lord, have mercy—(Hoop—hoop—hoop—) My God! but I didn't know that—(hoop—hoop—acheeach) Jesus, have mercy—I'm—(hoop—hoop—acheeach—) Great God, I—(hoop—hoop hoop—hock—kee—ach—kee,) my Lord!" he said. I never realized how good I had been until I heard how he was being punished. The Invisible Task Master seemed to have a wicked punch that landed right on the breadbasket every time, fouling according to the Queensbury rules, but nobody stopped HIM. Dejeuner turned out to be something good for my head—appetizing fruit, hot bread and coffee. Just what I used to straighten out my head on land when I felt bad. While eating, I learned there were a few other folks like myself that couldn't speak the new slang good. One lady at my table was having such a hard time I thought she might order the wrong thing and it would make her sick. So I went up on deck and watched Mother Nature build large cities and devour them in the heart of a wave: then she'd paint her beautiful landscapes with one stroke of her mighty brush. No artist has ever used water colors as she can.

The journey between the two lands was most refreshing, and it was exciting to me to realize, on the last day, that I was soon to put my foot on new ground. We docked at eleven o'clock in the morning. The way people there greeted the incoming passengers was grand—so joyously. Some were honored folks and they were kissed on both sides of the face.

I wasn't sure I was wanted there, the way the porters squealed like stuffed pigs because they didn't think the coin I gave them was large enough, although it was the same kind of a coin I gave the red caps at home for the same service rendered. In spite of their complaint, I found myself and my baggage cooped in a compartment of a little train that bounced through the country like a toy train in a kindergarten. Soon the cars stopped at the station in Paris. Men were lined up on the platforms in uniforms like cadets I have seen at home. A signal was given by someone, and they all rushed to the passengers, holding brass checks in their hands, crying like Amazon warriors of old when they were released in a band to pick their lovers. As we walked down the platform to the gate that led to the street, I could hear a dreadful noise being made outside of the high rock fence. Many tin horns were going *Toot-toot! Whee-whee! Blah-blah! Booa-booa!* I thought a lot of drunken folks from New York were celebrating their arrival in France like the way they celebrate the New Year when it comes in.

Once I got outside, you can imagine my surprise to see the street was jammed with toy cabs, to convey the new influx to their new domiciles. I had chosen a place from the news ad printed in the ship's paper, because I liked the figure back of it for the day rates. Someone told me I wouldn't need a special place at night in Paris. When I found out so many people made dreadful mistakes in trying to talk, I cut the ad out of the paper so that the people could read for themselves where I wanted to go. I showed it to the driver. He cried, *"Oui! Oui!"* and stepped on the gas.

In a few minutes, Johnson and I were in a small hotel not far from Eiffel's tower. We were going through the same routine I went through when I was in the workhouse—all but the fingerprints and the weighing in. A lady assigned me my room.

I hung up my clothes and prepared to shave that I might look keen when I appeared in the streets of Paris. I skinned down to my underwear, then I walked into the washroom. As I opened the door, my eyes reflected to my brain a new facility, a peculiar-shaped vessel setting in the corner of the room. I didn't pay much attention to it at first, and proceeded to shave. My mind was full of thoughts of how grand the hospitality and banquets must be in Paris, according to the way they served us on the boat coming over. After shaving, I started to wash my teeth, and I noticed the little sink in the bottom of the new vessel. My mind was set aspinning about what they used that thing for. In the middle of my thought, the lady that assigned my room came to the door with my receipt. I would have asked her what they used it for, but she looked too innocent, so I made up my mind to wait until I found someone that spoke slow French to find out. . . . I'll bet lots of people from

America make a big mistake the first time they use that
facility in Paris. . . .

After shaving and dressing, I came down into the hotel lobby. I noticed on a sign that the races were going
on that afternoon. The clerk told me I just had time to
catch the last three races at the Bois de Boulogne track.
A cab soon landed me in the milling mob about the
green. I had been to many great races and games at home,
but never did I see a place where everyone was betting
their money and not letting all hell know about it.

The people in Paris would empty the large grandstand
between the races like a fire drill in the public schools.
They went to the betting booths and put up their money.
Then just a few moments before the next race started,
the grandstand would fill up quickly again. The horses
were led to the post on a turf track. They ran backwards to most races I had seen in the West: they turned
to the right. At the start of a race, you'd hear a little
shout, "They're off!" like you might hear from a Boston
society group of people in an Art Theatre when the
comedian got his biggest laugh over. Then they would be
silent till the home stretch. Perhaps they would put up
about as much cheering noise as a Republican senator
would get in a Democratic House when he is introduc-
ing a bill. Thousands of francs are won and lost. I began
to think I was in paradise. From the races, I went to a
fine restaurant on the rue Pigall. Oh, the service—how
artful! I almost cried to think how I used to butcher that
kind of work.

Then for a short walk to the *Follies Bergere*. Work-

men were remodelling the front of the place, and it looked like the builders of the pyramids were in their prime again and had the job of beautifying the front of the noted theatre. Inside, it was as described to me. The show made me know where I was for the first time. It was the only place I had seen women put on the stage in their birthday suits, and they were not suggestive to even ruthless me. Perfect in art. The theatre was packed with Americans and a lot of good jokes went dead. I could tell by the way the French speaking people among them looked about the audience. During the intermission, I went down into the basement of the theatre, where East Indians did marvellous stunts to the tune of the old kootch dance. A black band with a white pianist played *Mississippi Blues* as we ascended the stairs to our last perspective of the heavenly settings and performers. The vivacious Josephine Baker was flopping her bananas like cowtails in fly time. I wished a lot of people who didn't like her at home could see her then.

After the show we went into the street, where men whispered into our ears, "We are the authorized guides to the Crystal Palace," and showed us pictures of the living sights to be seen there. Then came that feeling that comes once in a lifetime. Men in neat uniforms soliciting my trade to spend money for food and dance if I chose to. The image on the franc sitting on the throne half leaning on a musical instrument—he was no bogus bastard. If I rubbed his back, he could do anything I wanted him to do within reason.

I went back to the hotel, where I rang the front door

bell. I saw no one, but the large steel gates opened, the lights lit. I walked up into my room unseen and prepared for bed. Once again, as I started to wash my teeth, I was puzzled by the new vessel that sat in the corner of the washroom. If it was a place to wash my teeth, why not make it higher? And not so big. A foot tub? No, it wasn't big enough for that—at least mine. Besides, it was in an awkward place. You couldn't get a chair up to it handy. I went to sleep in hopes I might dream and see it used for the first time.

The next morning I set out to see all the sights in and around Paris, from the art museums to Louis XV's old hangouts. I rambled until the sun cut off the lights so that the tablets were no longer visible. The last I read that day was something about a German shell taking the head off a statue at the end of the Madeleine on May 30, in the year of our Lord, 1918. It was on May 30, 1927, that I lost my head over Paris.

CHAPTER 19

AN ISLAND IN HEAVEN

IN a short time, we sailed to England. It was on a Friday morning around 5:30 when we rode up to a hotel in dear old London. After getting our room and moving into it, I set out to find the charming actress, Florence Mills. She was playing at the Strand Theatre with her Blackbirds company at the time. The little lady was in her dressing-room. She had just returned from an affair with royalty. I was fortunate in knowing most of the people in the company, and I was sure to get the lowdown on the new land my feet had just struck. I was surprised to learn how quick most of the boys had received their degree as first class English interpreters. I could hardly understand their talk. When they were at home, they used to say "bin." It had been changed to "beeian" and "heah" was laid down for "heeare," and when they laughed, they couldn't get their mouths open. But I made them jar loose with a few fresh jokes from the sticks. Then we got on an understanding basis with each other.

That night we had front row seats at the performance of the Blackbirds. The show screamed the audience. After the show, we hit the streets again. . . . Never in my life have I seen so many people piling out of theatres. I said to the gang, New York was hot, Paris was a wampet cat, but London was the cat's kittens. Hardly had I time to get an answer before all the people disappeared like fiddler crabs on the beach when you walk among them. Restaurants closed up; only a few night clubs and cafés open in the Soho district. With a few friends, we had a fine midnight lunch . . . breast of Maryland fried chicken on toast, and all the good things that Italians know how to put with it. We washed the food down with fine Chianti. Many a person I had heard *talk* about good food—that night made me know it.

In the bright lights, we walked through Leicester Square, where the women of all nations parade in hopes of some lonely men asking them to accompany their party for a little lunch—any amount he might care to pay for it, from five shillings up to five pounds.

On the way to the Hotel, the further away from the Square we got, the darker it grew. I began to sour on "dear old Lun'nun," as most people called it. When I arrived at the hotel, it was locked up tight as a drum. It was forty minutes before I could get in. . . I am glad the King couldn't read my thoughts then, although the time wasn't long before I changed my song, after I learned the inside route of London. The people showed me the grandest time I had in Europe.

Our big send-off professionally was set by Somerset Maugham. He was the first person to engage us to sing in his home. He had in his drawing-room the cream of England to listen to us. The reception they gave us was the foundation of our success everywhere we sang in England. It was the first time in my life since I had been a man that I had met a large Group of Caucasians that really knew they were white and didn't feel that contact with an Ethiopian could taint their chastity. (I had lots of good friends in America who had proven themselves free, but seldom did I get in a big party that some thinskin didn't try to dig me, in what they thought was a clever crack about being black. Later on, I always found out they weren't sure about themselves.) I never shall forget that gathering. I was sure I was on the top of the mountain, because the faces and names were familiar to me of the people I had seen photos of and read their blooded pedigrees. I'll admit I was nervous enough at my first concert engagement, but never have I been so upset as I was at the beginning of this party. I wasn't bothered about my singing; it was these people that made it so different from any other society function I had attended. They were not afraid to talk to me, or ask me anything they thought I might know about. The women didn't have to have men standing by their sides to be at ease while we had a little chat.

I was introduced to Lady Oxford, one of the most fascinating, energetic ladies one would want to meet. After learning my name, the first question she asked me was, "Have you got a good black bottom?" Before I could answer, she turned to the lady sitting at the piano, not three feet from me, and said, "Play the music we dance our black bottom to." The lady struck up that syncopated melody of *ta*-tata-*ta*-tata, and Lady Oxford turned toward me with her eyes staring toward my feet, which remained motionless. When I didn't start to dance, she looked at me with great disappointment. "Oh, aren't you going to teach me your step?" she asked.

I was all balled up. I did want to show her my black bottom then, but you know I had gone to this party with singing on my mind, and to do the best I knew how. I said, "I am very sorry to disappoint you at the present time. I have been congratulated for having a good black bottom, but critics say singing spirituals is my specialty—although if you care to wait until later on, I will gladly display it."

She accepted the agreement and continued to talk. Her next question was, where did I come from. When I had given her that information she asked me what my first position in life was.

I got hot under the collar and kinda stuttered out, "I'd like to tell you, but I don't think a lady would be interested in it."

That seemed to fire her inquisitiveness. "Why, a lady wants to know everything under the sun! Out with it!" she said.

I swallowed laboriously and told her my first job was page in a sporting house.

"How thrilling! Phenominal! What a leap, from a Brothal to singing spirituals for Royalty! How did you bridge the gap?" she asked.

This question made me nervous, because I didn't know. The things I had read in the book of etiquette seemed to be guiding me wrong. The book said, never to stop talking abruptly to one person to talk to another, unless you begged to be excused. I stopped talking to Lady

Oxford because I couldn't answer her. The next thing I knew I was talking to Lady Astor's sister, when some one pulled me away from her to introduce me to Sacheverell Sitwell, without saying anything to either Lady Astor's sister or me. I would have remembered the Lady's name if it hadn't been so closely connected to Lady Astor. (You know Zora Hurston put *Astor-perious* in the Harlem slang, and that means the most elegant people on earth. Naturally, I was excited when I met these people face to face who were the cause of it being so defined.) I wished I had a picture of myself looking back at her like a little kid being dragged away from a candy shop window by his mother.

There was another thing made clear to me that night—how tall the majority of the English people are. I am six feet in my shoes and I was handicapped on the action of my brain while talking to these because I had to look up so much. If it hadn't have been for the nervous strain and delicious champaign I drank that evening, I don't think I would have slept a wink for trying to figure out this world and the people in it.

* * *

Once we were comfortably located in an apartment on South Hampton Road, I made up my mind to see the city and playgrounds of the old Kings. For eight months, I investigated their hangouts in my spare time. Ah, what a devilish lot they were! Few of them were weaklings or loathed the fair sex. They would cut the head off of their best pal if they wanted his voluptuous wife and think nothing of it. Then the majority of people still believe in the laws they have handed down.

One of the sights I saw while passing a Pub interested me. Of course you know all the Pubs in London have first, second and third-class stalls for people of different classes. A high-class man wouldn't think of going into a cheap man's stall—neither would a poor person go into a first-class stall or anywhere his money didn't fit. I was going over to see Turner Layton of Layton and Johnston, America's most popular entertainers in England, who lived on Doughty Street. I had to pass up High Holborn to get to Doughty Street from Southampton Row. There must be at least a dozen Pubs between the two streets. As I passed one, the usual mob was packed in it. The kids were playing in the hallways while their mothers and fathers enjoyed their 'alf and 'alf. I stopped to light a cigarette in front of the place, and while doing so, I heard a lady say in a quite aristocratic tone of voice, to a lady a little her senior:

"So you know my boy, do you?"

"Yes, 'indeed, I do know him," the elder lady answered.

"Well, 'ow long 'ave you been knowing 'im?" the young lady asked.

"Ah, it's a long time," the elderly lady said, following up with a question to the young lady, " 'ow long 'ave *you* been knowing Derek?"

"Ah, I've been knowing 'im since school days," the young lady said.

"You don't say! Well, would you believe it when I tell you I've been knowing 'im before that? Do you know 'is mother put 'im in my baby carriage when she went out on business?" the senior lady said.

"I don't believe it! My boy never associated with the likes of you," the young lady said.

"Why, that's an insult. You've insulted me! Don't think because I'm drinking beer 'ere in a lowly pub, I didn't come from the 'igher class? You 'ave *insulted* me," the old lady said.

"I'll do more than that, I'll box your face," the young lady said.

"That's a challenge! I'll show my quality. I'll accept it. Come out 'ere in the street," the old lady said, leading the way.

The whole pub emptied except the bar-maids. Most of the people held their drinks, and sauntered out talking to one another like a business man's meeting breaking up. Before the old lady could get her coat off, the young lady grabbed her. They both went around and around. Somehow in the tousle the old lady went down flat on her stomach, all stretched out. The young lady walked up and kicked her in the ribs. *Whamm*, it sounded. The old lady raised up on her arms, straightened out full length! She looked like her back was broken at the hip joints. She turned her head sideways looking up at the young lady, who had backed away three or four feet. "Ah; as I thought! As I thought! You are not a blooded lady—you don't play fair," the old lady said. Some other women intervened and they all went back into the pub and had a drink together. The old lady clicked her glass on the glass of her opponent, and said in a dignified manner, "I'm of the 'igher class. Royal blood will tell," she said, and I walked on.

It struck me later the old lady was right. I couldn't conceive the idea of two great artists both being on exhibition at the same time like the King and Crown Prince are so many times together, without the senior one of the two getting hinkty, if the junior one got too much of a hand. I was within twenty feet of the King, Queen, and Crown Prince, when it looked like all of Europe and half of America had turned out to see the great ceremony of giving away the new colors to the King's guard. You can say what you please about Kings and Queens, there is something about them that makes your blood tingle any time you see them struting their stuff. Old King George!—Now while I have seen men at home that were great, they never had that nonchalent stand that let you know he knew he himself was the ripe nuts and coffee without telling you how much the dinner cost. King George is that kind of a man. He can put on a stand that is too bad, saying nothing of his commands. I would like to live to see some spade in that kind of a performance some day. Hot Dog! . . . Then dig my grave.

Then when the Queen is out, I have only seen one woman in the U. S. A. that equalled her when she was entertaining the blue-bloods of Manhattan. When the Queen rode by me that day, sitting in her car, her haughty back never touched the cushion. . . . Straight as an arrow! As soft as that black cushion looked, most anyone else would have used it. That pleasing little smile on her face is not just quite the real hearty smile I would like to see there. I thought I'd like to take her up in the heart-a-the Rocky Mountains some warm August day and tell her stories . . . maybe I'd get the effect I'd like.

And say, you should have heard the mob shout and scream when the King passed, riding a Chestnut bay horse. The horse pranced along with a well bowed neck, as if he knew he was carrying precious cargo and spirit was the thing to be—but not dangerously active, or he might lose it. But when His Royal Highness, the Prince came by, on a horse that bounced sideways and backwards, like his legs were made of giant springs and that was the only way he could move . . . bounce along! . . . That mob! Never in my life have I heard such cutting up, each group picking up as the Prince appeared, like a chain of fire-crackers on one fuse.

And the King's band on horse-back! If you ever intend to call yourself living, see the King's band on horseback. Every horse is jet black except the one that carries the Gold Kettle Drums in front. He's an Arabian Pinto with large black, white and brown spots on him. There is one horse that it's a pity he can't talk. And the man that·rides him knows his Jones. They were playing a lively march when they passed me. I was within ten feet of the Drum Horse. *Baump* . . . *tee dee baump* . . . *tee* . . *dee* . . *baump* . . . *baump*, the drums played. And the horse danced like a rhymetical loving tropical native would keep time with the music. I thought of all the cruelty of all the old Kings, but if their way of living led up to giving people as much of a thrill as I got out of that day, they were justified in committing any kind of a crime to get the effect. It made me feel like . . . oh, it made me feel like it . . . it . . . oh, I can't tell you what it made me feel like.

Then on my travels through the country in England, I saw peculiar ways to build cities. In some towns, the houses and streets looked so much alike I couldn't understand how a man lit up could find his way home at night.

I was greatly disturbed by the clamorous appeal the churches made there, to get people to attend their holy meetings. These bells are a beautiful thing to hear, but it's only in an English town like Harrogate or Bristol that you can really understand the different opinions about how to get to Heaven. The way the clarions ring at eleven o'clock on a Sunday morning, there are no words to express. Just imagine forty churches all with a good set of from four to sixteen bells each, ringing out their individual appeal at once. As I laid in that soft bed at the hotel and listened to their dissention, I realized it was time to write a new Bible for two or three reasons. First, many men had shown too much light on the stories in the Bible. Second, few people could, if they wanted to, live up to the agreements they secretly made with their God, on account of the modern conditions. So why not twelve people, men and women, sit down and write us a new book of stories, so that those that believe in them can live up to them? Why not write the mythological doctrine so no scientist can pick it to pieces and bring out any part of the core? Writers like Judge Ben Lindsay, G. B. Shaw, H. G. Wells, Rebecca West, Fannie Hurst, H. L. Mencken, Heywood Broun, Theodore Dreiser, Elinor Glyn, King Vidor, Charlie Chaplin, Prof. C. K. Ogden, Carl Van Vechten and Gertrude Stein. And this time they must put the music to the songs in the New Bible, and the notes must never be changed. Then when people hear the melody set to beautiful words like:

"Let him kiss me with the kisses of his mouth, for thy love is better than wine.

"Because of the savour of thy good ointments, thy name is as ointment poured forth. Therefore do the virgins love thee. Draw me: we will run after thee.

"The King hath brought me into his chambers: we will be glad and rejoice in thee; we will remember thy love more than wine. The upright love thee.

"I am black, but comely, O ye daughters of Je-ru-sa-lem, as the tents of Kedar, as the curtains of Solomon." they will know the musicians are playing a sacred piece, and not a crowd-getting for a prohibition meeting. Max Ewing should set this to music.

I am sorry there is no one that could write that part about the devil, though if there must be some black man in the gang, I don't think anyone would give him a squarer deal than myself. Of course, if some black Moses leads his people up on higher ground, he's going in the gang, too! However, I am not looking for any odd numbers.

One thing that must go in the next Bible, and the League of Nations must swear by with utmost sincerity, is that only one portrait of the Saviour can be painted, and all copies must be an exact duplicate. I noticed in my ramblings through the few great galleries in the world I had been in, that almost every race or nation but mine has had a great painter to paint a portrait of Jesus Christ with features like themselves. They say there is a black Jesus Christ portrait in the Hermitage at Moscow, or some place in Sweden. I don't know, but if I can ever afford it, I'll find out. In the meantime, I command a Negro artist to get busy at once and do a portrait of Christ with broad nose and slightly favoring his people.

* * *

Next we were invited to a dinner party by Lady Trowbridge and Radclyffe Hall, the writers, two very very interesting people—so singular. Lady Trowbridge is what I always had in mind an English Lady should be like. I can't say why any particular contour of the face and body should have come to me to be what a native of any country should be like, but she fills the bill on the female side. Radclyffe Hall is equally as striking, and the kind of person that is always so attractive in her manner. At that dinner party, in their beautiful Chelsea District home, I got the thrill of my life. (By the way, they have the most beautiful small sunken garden I have ever seen at the back of their house—all kinds of flowers, a small lake with colored lights on the bottom so you can see the goldfish of all shades at night. Their little bull terrier trapsing around the green lawn makes everything glow with bubbling life. It's too grand.) There were ten of us who sat down to a delicious dinner—Lady Trowbridge at one end of the table and Radclyffe Hall at the other. I sat next to Radclyffe, and John Galsworthy sat across from me. Robert Burton Cunningham Grahame was there too, and we got into a conversation. It seems he had ridden on horseback through my home state, Montana, as well as up the steps of Buckingham Palace. He is a double of Buffalo Bill. If he had been a little taller, I would have sworn Buffalo Bill wasn't dead. Sir Robert and I were having the time of our lives reminiscensing our trips through the Little Big-horn, and around Black Butte, into the bad lands of the West on spirited horses. For a time, we were almost unaware of anyone else being at the table with us. Radclyffe broke up our intense interest and we noticed we had been a bit selfish.

When dinner was over, we all gathered in the music room that soon filled up with a lot of people who came in after the theatres were closed. Ursula Greville, who can sing old Irish and Scotch Folklore better than anyone I have ever heard, held all spellbound, and our spirituals were well received.

These concerts and private musicals increased our popularity. We were soon engaged to sing at the Coliseum, the world's largest variety house. I had spent three years in America's vaudeville, but never before in any place where they had a revolving stage. Three big acts can be set up at one time. When one act closes, they just whirl the next one around before the audience. Lady Oxford's words popped into my mind, "Thrilling! Phenominal!" I got so excited when the stage rolled so fast I almost forgot what I was to show—my ability to sing or my black bottom. When we had finished our act, the people in the audience began to call for their favorite songs. One lady shouted, "Sing *Go Way, Moses.*" Another, "*Poor Old Joe!*" and some man in the gallery called out for *You got Boots and I got Boots.* I wondered why these people shouted to us to sing strange songs when we were listed as "Negro Spiritual Singers." Mr. Johnson and I glanced at each other and sang, *Go Down, Moses.* The first lady almost clapped her hands off, she was so pleased. Evidently that was what she wanted. *Poor Old Joe* turned out to be *Old Black Joe; You got Boots and I got Boots* was substituted for *All God's Chilluns Got Wings.*

At the close of our act, a friend sent for me to meet him in the theatre. I arrived just in time to be served tea and see the last two acts. Seated next to us were some people enjoying high-balls. If old Volstead could have known what I was thinking of, he would have me locked up. I realized Americans might earn more money, but damned if they get so much out of life. During that week, the theatre was packed. It was Bank Holiday week. The English people have some kind of a holiday every day. One time it's the tailor, the next the grocer, and so on until every dog has his day.

Another thing I noticed, in the big hotels in London you see white-haired men with chicks or an old lady with a young man. To me, it looked like fathers and daughters, or mother and son, but their actions told me my opinion must be wrong regarding their family relations. Whatever their connections were, they seemed to have the right idea, because they got along so well.

I was very sad to think I had to leave before I could learn all about the country, and I knew that would take a long time. Our management wired for us to come home. You can never know how I felt. I was thirty-four years old and had only lived eight months since I left home. I don't know what I did do to get such a punishment. I had to jump from London to Louisville, Kentucky. Few spades have paid that debt with a smile.

CHAPTER 20

BACK HOME

W HEN I landed in New York, a man met me at the pier with a queer remark. Instead of him saying, I am glad to see you, he grabbed my hand and said, "Be good, now; be good."

I could tell by the color of his face he was not thinking of what I was thinking of. "Be good. Be good about what?" I said.

"Don't bother the women. You are in America now," he said.

"Must I turn drag, eh? Is that the way a 100 percent American wants to threaten me, a black American, because he thinks my black body might have been parked nude next to some white woman. . . There are plenty of black women in Europe, you know," I said.

The redness of his face turned to its natural color. "I never thought about that," he said. . . .

We only spent two nights in New York City before going West. I was glad to see old Harlem again, but I think we could have remained away from Harlem longer without crying to return. I hadn't made a bet of any kind except on a few races in Paris since I left America. I felt my break was about due for a win. One night, I went into Jock's club to meet the gang and play a hand with the boys. The place was full of men and women—mostly men. There are a few women that can stand to play table stakes with the men in Harlem, and it looked like they all were there with their cast iron nerve registering two below zero. We all exchanged greetings and they asked me about my trip. All I said was, "Folks, if I told you the truth, you'd tell me to stop lying." Then the players fell into their regular conversational story-telling. Ever since the prudy ladies have ruined the barber shops for stories, the only place that seems to be left for exchange is the poker club, and it looks like they are going to kill them off there. I can't mention all the names of the people in the club that night, so I'll refer to a person in the game as a player and the rest as the gang.

One of the players, a doctor, began, "Ha-ha-ha! I'll be damned if a niggah ain't a funny thing. You know, I don't make any more night calls unless its an old patient of mine, or unless someone is next to death. Well, the other night about three A. M., the 'phone rang. My wife answered it. It was an old friend of mine, but I had never known this spade to be sick. His wife was talking: she said her husband was very ill, and she wanted me to come down right away. I told my wife to try and find out what his complaint was and to tell her I'd be down as soon as I came in. His wife said this niggah was hilarious and she couldn't quiet him down. My wife hung up and I went to sleep again. I had to make a six o'clock call and I thought I'd kill the two birds with the same stone. Well, sir! in about an hour the 'phone rang again. It was this niggah's old lady, saying her husband had gotten worse and she must have a doctor right away. I got up and got the car and drove down to this darky's house. He was sitting up in the middle of the bed, hollering, 'Hee! Hee! Hee!'

"I said, 'Calm yourself, man; calm yourself.' Then this zigaboo did perform. I had to give him a shot of morphine to quiet him down so I could examine him. Do you know what was the matter with that Jasper? He had gone into some kind of a manufacturing business with two other inks and they had appointed him treas-urer and, like a dam' fool, he used his own checking ac-count. That morning he got a letter from the bank with a turned down check, 'No Funds.' So when this spade tried to find the other two hucks they couldn't be found anywhere, and the reaction had just set in on him at four o'clock in the morning. I could have killed that dumb Oscar. . . Yes, yes; I'll see it. Three kings and two jacks."

"Damn them funny stories, Doc—and winnin' my money," one of the players said.

"Men do hate to pay for amusement," a lady in the game said.

"Men like to win their amusement."

"Say, Gordon! Give me your first play on the num-bers for good luck from Europe." This was said by a collector.

"Sure—put 179 on for me—the number of my state-room I had coming back on the boat," I answered him.

The next morning, the number hit in the gate: *Bamm!* If I'd had eight or ten dollars on it at six hundred to one, I would have taken the next boat back to Europe. Instead, I went west to Louisville, Kentucky, for a concert. The three days' old smoke with a peculiar tart aroma of burnt human flesh was still in the air. . . It was on a Sunday afternoon, December the 22nd, when we sang spirituals on the Brown's Theatre stage in Louisville, not far from my mother's birthplace. I called her out of the grave to sing the songs for the people that once held her in bondage. A queer electric halo seemed to hover over the audience, as they listened to dead slaves, whose forms seep through walls, ceilings and windows—a thousandfold—to sing the Christian fables to their pagan melodies and rhymes. After the concert they waved their webby forms back to their bones to rest in the grave, until they are needed again. . . . Slaves right on, and always shall be slaves, as long as pagans can concentrate.

From Kentucky I went north, making many stops on my old stamping grounds. One of the greatest laughs in my life came to me in a little town in Minnesota. The women that sponsored the concert there made reservations for us to stop at one of the best hotels in the city. When we arrived to take up our reservations, the lady back of the counter became deaf and dumb. Her actions would have been worth a million to some movie actress. I was so amused. When she did mumble out some words it seemed she had found all the rooms in the vacant hotel filled by telegram reservations ahead. We went about phoning, trying to get a place to stop. The three ladies who were running the concert came in to see if we were comfortably fixed. When they found out we had no reservations, they had a fit. The lobby had ten or twelve men sitting in the big front window looking out, with their ears as long as jackasses, listening to what was going on at the desk, ten or twelve feet back of them.

Finally, the three ladies left in a body, as if they were going to leave us to our fate. They went across the street and got a big Packard car and drove it up in front of the hotel; then one of them came into the lobby and told us to get our baggage, and go home with them. We all piled in the car and drove off. Just before dinner the doctor who owned the house where we were stopping came home. His wife started to tell him what happened; he cut her off by throwing his hands in the air and saying, "Tut tut—I know. I have just come from the hotel, and the discussion down there for the last hour has been, 'What is the best? Let those damn niggers stay here in this hotel where we can watch 'em, or let them go with those three white women, where we *can't* watch 'em," he said.

At the doctor's house we had a fine room and a delicious dinner. If it hadn't been for their courageous hospitality I might have felt half sore at the town, and not done my best at the concert; but to think I had them guessing about my actions! . . . Louis the Fifteenth in his palmy days never cut up any more than I did that night. There has been few places where we have gotten bigger receptions. Then we came on back east.

On the train I was sitting in my berth reading the newspaper. A lady passed me by going to the diner and she kinda nodded to me as if she knew me. I nodded back, but I did not pay much attention to her, not placing her as one of my many acquaintance. After she had her dinner she came back and sat in the berth with me.

"I enjoyed your concert very much at Orchestra Hall in Chicago," she said.

I thanked her and we continued to talk. The conversation jumped from one topic to another. She told me she was going to Monte Carlo to get a divorce, and an artist had told her that since Isadora Duncan was dead, she was the only woman that could take her place. She thought herself quite lucky because of her close contact with Gurdjieff . . . her success as an artist would be COLLOSSAL. I looked her over from head to foot. While her figure was quite in her favor, the contour of her face was somewhat against her; then besides, for my idea of the Venus that Isadora's successor should look like, this lady did not fill all the requirements, although she seemed to be a charming person. I was to see her in New York that evening, to take her to the Dark Tower and other interesting places in Harlem, but when I got home I was so busy straightening out old obligations I missed the bewitching lady.

I hadn't been in New York but two days when we had to go down on Park Avenue to entertain some of New York's bluebloods. After the affair, I was going home when a fellow met me with the regular Harlem greeting, "Hello Bo. Where you going? Madge is giving a rent party tonight. You better drop in. All the pretty browns in town'll be there." I told him I might. I went home and wrote a few letters and changed my dress suit. Never wear a dress suit to a rent party. It will be in your way.

In Harlem most of the flat rents are so high some people can't make the monthly payments, so when they are pushed real close they tell all their friends to come over, and to bring all their friends they know to be O. K. When these people arrive they drop any amount of money into the box at the door from a half dollar up. Seldom more than one dollar. The landlady or gentleman that might be behind in his rent sells chittlings, pigs feet or chicken salad, hot dogs and drinks. Some of the guests furnish the music in relay, so there are always enough piano-thumpers to keep the party going, inspired by the vital and loving dancers.

This night I dropped my money in the box at 1:05 A. M. Someone was playing a slow drag. The front room to the railroad flat was a moving mass of swaying bodies doing the bump as I entered. I saw a tall black gal two shades darker than vici kid, dressed in a green velvet dress with the back cut V shape down to her hips. She had perfect caucasian features and Walkerized hair—a treat for any eye to see. Two beautiful pearl earrings hung on a three-inch gold chain from her ears. Legs like champaign bottles. She sure is one black woman that knows how to dress. Her willowy form was hanging around a tall collegiate's neck, swaying to and fro like a leaf in a breeze.

I walked through to the back room, parked my blanket and skypiece on the bed, and got back to the parlor just as this dame was loosening her holt as the music was dying out.

"Hay Beau, make me acquainted with the queen," I said to her partner.

"No use, Buddie, no use—you need target practice," the collegiate answered me. They laughed as they passed me going to the kitchen where the drinks were sold. I followed. He made me known to the fair creature. Many a hot shot was fired over drinks. The evening went on. One warm party . . . a couple here and there going home every now and then. Around three forty, there were four of us men and eight or ten women left in the place. We men were like a lot of tom cats on the back fence when the she cat is on the ground—waiting for a chance to jump down with tales of love. I had never seen such a charming woman at a rent party before. Finally (she had been out of the room for some reason for a few moments) we were all telling our best lies, amusing ourselves. The girls were all signifying nothing freakish, when the Queen came back into the room with an interrupting ejaculation, "Get out, you long horns! I am the visiting Queen, and I am closing my den," she said. I was dazed and didn't move.

The other fellows started for their coats and hats. I looked around the room and said to myself, this woman might be the horned toad's daughter, but I can't see how she can entertain all these women handy, and I intended to stay. She brought me my hat and coat and threw them at me. "You too, singer", and with her assistance I was helped out of the house. All four of us fellows walked down Lenox Avenue discussing our bad judgment. We agreed the lady was too deep for us. She is the fourth dimension.

A very great lady writer had sent me her latest publication a few days previous to this. When they do such a nice thing I always write a letter of thanks to the author, and put in my latest episode, if it can be told at all. I was delighted I had not written her before this happened, because I did not think I had anything fresh at hand so good. I thought all writers were alike, and they get some color out of such a story, so I put it in my letter. I have never known just what the lady thought, but I have an idea. I lost her friendship for a long while but she forgave me. I am glad because I hate to lose friends.

Ever since I have been enjoying life in and around New York, most of the time I spend in Harlem, where the everyday life is one big drama, with plenty of mirth as well as its sad parts—especially around where I live. One night I had just gotten into my room when I heard screams in the street. I went out to see what was wrong. I learned a woman around thirty-eight years old had been keeping a man for some time, but of late he had been kinda running out on her. She found out he was keeping company with a little girl about eighteen, and they used to meet in the gin mill near me, known as The Sawdust Trail, before they went to their Love Nest. Usually they split up there, too. This night, the big brown knew they were out together, and she made up her mind to lay for them and beat the little gal up, so she hid back of the door under the steps—a place for the ashcans. She let the little gal go in the ginny and come out with her man. Then she jumped on the little gal. The little gal hollered "Murder!" and ran up 136th Street and turned north up Seventh Avenue faster than Drew could have made it.

After the little gal disappeared, the big brown hopped onto the man. She threw him away for fair—talked all about his business. She told him he never had a decent suit of clothes until he met her. The man said, "Shut up". She said, "Shut up? Shut up? Shut up?" three times. "You tell *me* to shut up? No, indeed. I'll tell the world that I—" *BAMM!* The man slapped her down. She got up very coy and sweet. She said, "Why, honey! You do care for me, don't you? You men sure are funny. I can't understand what you men want with these little chippies. They ain't no woman what knows what love is all about until she's at least thirty." Well, you shoulda heard the women in the mob that gathered say, "Ain't it the truth!"

Some of the events I wished everyone could see in Harlem, are the Fashion Shows and the Drag Balls and a few Society Dances. Nowhere else in the world do they stage dances like these. At the fashion show they have all of Harlem's beauties for manikens and they run in color from jet black to swansdown white, and the audience is the same. There is no way to write of the beautiful sight of this group on the dance floor after the show. Most of the dressmakers are employed by New York's richest people, and lots of these folks come to see the dusty seamstress put their touch to the Paris Gowns.

The drag dances are staged by men from Kansas City to New York who think they can make women look up and take notice, and really some of them would fool many a fly shiek if they were permitted to walk Broadway the way they look at the ball. They pay as high as $500 for their gowns to wear in the famous Harlem Drag Balls. These men are of all nations, white and black.

The last big ball I attended where these men got got the most of the prizes for acting and looking more like ladies than the ladies did themselves, was at the Savoy in Harlem. I had to call up everyone I thought hadn't been to one. On the day of the dance I got so many phone calls asking for tickets, I thought I was the president of the club sponsoring the affair. That night the hall was packed with people from bootblacks to New York's rarest bluebloods. The management picked Robert Chanler and a young lady writer (who is married to a millionaire I haven't met yet) and I to be the judges. The show that was put on that night for a dollar admission, including the privilege to dance, would have made a twenty-five dollar George White's *Scandals* opening look like a side show in a circus. You should have seen the expressions on fastidious womens' faces, when they learned such charming looking women were men. One beautiful lady said, "Well, if this keeps up, real women are going to have a battle that will be hard to beat. Look at the privilege these folks have!"

Bob Chanler took great delight in watching the mental impressions. He is one of the grandest, big-hearted men one would ever want to meet and can get more fun out of other people's actions than any person I know. He is positive of his individuality in everything, especially his paintings. He takes great pleasure in painting people's portraits in a clear tonality out of tune with the vibration of his subject, who would like to have their most fascinating points out on canvas. To me his work has the same effect on my brain that futuristic music has. They are beautiful if you understand them, and you could if you knew Robert Chanler. He knows and entertains people from all parts of the globe. They never forget him. In painting his portraits he paints the major thought of the subject at the time of the sitting. If you chance to be wearing a coat and your thoughts were more on the position of the coat than your facial expression, he would almost paint you featureless with a perfect coat. Still you would recognize the person if you knew them, by some one outstanding feature, like his painting of Carl Van Doren's eyes, and Louise Helstrom's hair, or the neck of Emily Vanderbilt.

One of the most glorious days I ever spent with Chanler was the day he painted Carl Van Vechten's portrait. I went down with Carl for his sitting. He wore a phantom red New Mexican cowboy shirt, with an orange and green bandanna handkerchief around his neck to pose in. Chanler likes for his subject to have guests and to talk all they please, but at least sit quiet for a few minutes. That day Carl was like a boy with the itch for some reason. He bobbed up and down like a robin on a green lawn in Springtime. Bob laughed and talked, squinted his eyes, pushed out his lips and painted. The first fifteen minutes was tough sledding. That red shirt seemed to blur everything, even the contour of Carl's forehead. Then they rested, drank a few cocktails and hit at it again.

Finally, the features began to take on a keen resemblance of Carl Van Vechten. Suddenly I saw Bob squint his eyes unusually tight, spread his closed lips that made his broad smile more characteristic, and hold his brush up like a player in a bullseye dart game. *Bang, bang*, the brush shot forth and put the image of Carl's two prominent front teeth in: a few other lines were drawn and Carl jumped up for a rest. After he stretched his legs and wet his throat, he looked at his portrait. Chanler laid down his brush and large palette, then took the painting out of the easel. He carried it into the large drafting room next to the studio where he put it into a frame on the wall. Then we all took seats twenty feet away from it, where we drank and criticized the work. Carl decided he didn't want the teeth in. I wanted to ask him why, but something told me not to. Why Carl, who has let other artists put their impression of his teeth on canvas, wouldn't let Bob Chanler paint them, will always be a mystery to me, especially after seeing Chanler's portrait of him.

Bob Chanler proves to me that he is a real Mister

Eddie, when he puts on his parties—which is nearly every night. He hates to be alone and the mob downstairs whooping it up seem to give him energy to paint. I must say he gets a great kick out of them. (But not often like the kick he got out of his impression of why Carl didn't want him to paint his teeth.) Every time I go down there he asks me questions about colored people. When he learned that Charles Gilpin, the actor, laid his downfall to Southern trainmen putting him out of a Pullman, he cried. He said he thought Gilpin was one of the world's greatest actors.

He has always been very much interested in my people. Not the kind of interest you would expect a real Southerner to have.

CHAPTER 21

ALL THE MILK AND HONEY I CAN GET

IF anyone has the idea in their minds that only Yankees are for the advancement of the Negro, please get it out. Experience has taught me different. I have found the whole obsessed idea has been built up on a theory that all black people are the last living substitutes for the long dead centaurs, and that seducing women is the only thing they think about. But close observation has taught me that the obnoxious trait is well grounded in all men, regardless of creed or color, only one group seem to be better equipped than the other, and all their eyes are much larger than their stomachs. You know anyone is subject to change their mind. The people that call themselves Southerners in America have caused me to lose plenty of sleep trying to figure them out.

Being dark complected, I must say a Southerner can be much more unpleasant in the South than he is in the North, but in Europe he is a darling. I'll admit that down south there is a set of ignorant people who would like to run all of the Negroes back to Africa. But they are held down by the folks behind the closed doors, better known to all colored people as Mister Eddie and Miss Ann. If it wasn't for these people, the Negro couldn't live in the South at all.

You may be surprised to learn that there is a certain

type of new immigrant to this country who are the Negro's worst enemy. They are quicker to turn him down for food or lodging than Americans. They come here with the idea that white Americans won't patronize them if a Negro is anywhere around: they use their own countrymen even to do their scrub-work.

I know many blueblooded Southerners who are helping the black people in many ways to get out of the rut. If the Negro could help himself as much as some Southerners try to help him, there wouldn't be any race question in the South.

I'll admit it has been the most incomprehensible subject or state of being that I have met in my life, and it would afford me great pleasure if I could meet face to face and talk to the originator of that much prattled about topic. Maybe it's not a person—just circumstances.

I knew I was black and different in appearance from most of the kids I played with, but my being so never changed the values of the game we might be playing. I got a chance to pitch or bat at the time my merits won for me either of the positions. It was Colored people that put the fear of nature in my head. I wonder if they would have had this fear in their hearts if they had been given the chance to play the game of life that I had had in playing ball? They made me believe that nothing but things pertaining to Whites were advantageous. White skin or straight hair would greatly increase my position, regardless of what was in my head.

233

It took me a long time to learn that that was the worst form of imprisonment.

When I think of the marvellous people I have met, and of my happy childhood days, free to associate with many nationalities, colors and creeds without being classed as an obnoxious Indian lover or Chinese lover, and that they have been free to associate with whom they chose, including myself, without being thrown out as a Nigger lover, I say to myself, What a lucky bird I am to have been laid on top of the Rocky Mountains, hatched out by the Broiling Sun, a suckling of Honey Bluebacks and educated by the Grizzly Bear, with all the beauty and fresh air Nature can provide for her children.

No wonder the Race Question has never been the big ghost in my life!

My stumbling blocks have been my inability to earn the amount of money I would like to have, which is nothing, and win the love I would like to have, that seems to be everything. I don't think I will ever call myself a success in life until I can move both of these stones. For me, there is no second best, even though for folks at home, when I was a kid, love meant everything. Now I know that the greatest kick in my life will be when I reach the point where I have joined finance with love. So far, I have found the problem next to solving the perpetual motion machine. When I have finance, I can't find love: then when I find love, I am usually broke. And I'm not happy with either of them alone.

If I had a movie-tone of my actions on the road I have travelled so far, I would be willing to go back to the mountains, surround myself with wine, women and song, and spend the rest of my days. But I haven't got it, and I'm still a poor man, so I must keep on, with the world's greatest celebrities, artists, musicians, writers, bull-dikers, hoboes, faggots, bankers, sweetbacks, hotpots, and royalty, who have framed my mind so that life goes on for me, one thrill after another—too many to mention. Thanks to Fate for teaching me the fundamental laws that I may live within this world and enjoy all the milk and honey I can get.

Ho! Ho! . . . I wonder what I was born to be?

GLOSSARY

CHINOOK: A warm wind occurring during the cold season.

SOOCK: Salt for cattle.

SWEETBACK: Professional male lover.

HOTPOT: A lewd woman.

PECKERWOOD: A poor white man.

CHIVAREE: Serenading a wedding.

INKS, JIGWALK, SPADE, HUCK, ZIGABOO, DINGE, JASPER; Nicknames for Ethiopians.

JIVE: A misleading remark.

MISS ANN and MISTER EDDIE: Emancipated bluebloods.

GIG: Entertaining with music.

BULL-DIKER: A woman who prefers her own sex.

ACE: A senior railroad porter.

In the *Blacks in the American West* series

SHADOW AND LIGHT: AN AUTOBIOGRAPHY
by Mifflin W. Gibbs

BORN TO BE
by Taylor Gordon

THE LIFE AND ADVENTURES OF NAT LOVE
by Nat Love

7112